MORE REDDITCH
REMEMBERED

MORE
REDDITCH
REMEMBERED

ALAN FOXALL

AND

RAY SAUNDERS

First published in Great Britain in 2007 by
The Breedon Books Publishing Company Limited
Breedon House, 3 The Parker Centre,
Derby, DE21 4SZ.

This paperback edition published in Great Britain in 2013 by DB
Publishing, an imprint of JMD Media Ltd

ISBN 978-1-78091-347-6

Printed and bound in the UK by Copytech (UK) Ltd Peterborough.

CONTENTS

ACKNOWLEDGEMENTS

The authors would like to thank the following people for their help in compiling this, the second volume of images of bygone Redditch. Much of the material comes from their own archives collected over the last few decades with additional photography by Alan Foxall. However, many of the pictures belong to others in the locality who have generously allowed us to copy their own collections of family photographs and postcards. Unfortunately some names may inadvertently be omitted due to the long time scale and the filing system – or lack of it – particularly when filed only in the memory. Diane Adams, the Beck family, Tim Bicknell, Anne Bradford, Terry Burton, Alison and Derek Case, Roy Davies, Mrs Ellis, Jack Harper, John Harris, Ian Hayes, Peter Hemming, Philip Jarvis, Pat Lee, John Lewis, Mr and Mrs Louch, John Maries, Norman Neasom, Alan Quiney, John Rattue, Maureen Saunders, Mark Saunders, Jill Smith, John Stroud, Karen Ryman and John Whitmore.

The authors would especially like to thank Mike Cater for the loan of his photographs of his father, well-known demolition contractor Ernie Cater, at work in the town in the 1950s, 60s and 70s.

INTRODUCTION

The first volume of *Redditch Remembered* has proved to be so popular that it has had to be reprinted and because of its success we have been asked to produce another book along similar lines. We received many favourable comments from people who read the book. It brought back happy memories to many of a mature age and provided a glimpse of what Redditch used to be to the young people of the town.

The town of today is totally different from the town of 40 years ago. The Redditch Development Corporation tore the heart out of 'old Redditch' with very little being done to preserve its industrial and social heritage. It not only swept away the shops, offices and factories where people worked, but also the places such as church halls, the Kingfisher Hall and most of the pubs and clubs where they could meet and relax after work. The Fleece Inn, Hungry Man, Nag's Head, Plumber's Arms, Rifleman, Rising Sun and the Talbot all disappeared and the existing social network was destroyed.

Since the 1960s many of the old established town industries have gone, firms like Royal Enfield, Terry's Springs, Milwards, Alkaline Batteries and most of the needle and fishing tackle factories are no more. Their demise was mostly due to outside influences like foreign competition; however, more could surely have been done to preserve at least some of the historic factory complexes like Washford Mill and the Lodge Road works, refurbishing and modernising their interiors for use as light industry or offices as has been done to some extent with Millsbro House.

Perhaps if the New Town Development was being planned now instead of 1964 things might be done differently, with the main centre out of town and a pedestrianised Evesham Street.

Those who are entrusted with running a town must realise that Heritage IS important. It gives the place its character and provides a certain status. People feel proud to belong to the town and are saddened when they see changes that are not always for the best.

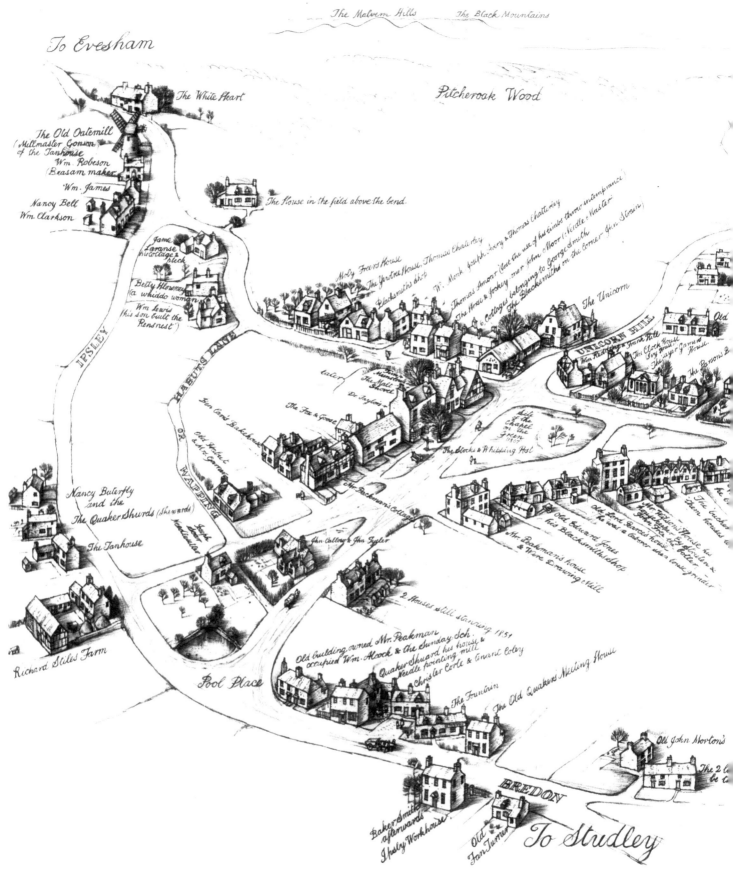

The Malvern Hills   The Black Mountains

To Evesham

The White Hart

Pitcheroak Wood

The Old Oatemill
(Millmaster Gonson
of the Tanhouse
Wm. Robeson
(Beasam maker
Wm. James
Nancy Bell
Wm. Clarkson

The House in the field above the bend.

Jame Laranse
his cottage &
plech

Betty Holloway
a whiddo woman

Wm Lewis
(his son built the
Rensnest)

IPSLEY

Holy Freers House

The Yewtree House, Thomas Chaterley

Blacksmith's shop

Wm. Monk, Joseph Avery & Thomas Chatterley

Thomas Amour (lost the use of his limbs throw intemperance
The Horse & Jockey, mr. John Moor (. Needle & Waster

6. Cottages belonging to George Smith
The Blacksmiths on the Corner, Jhn Stoun

The Unicorn

UNICORN HILL

Wm Restall, Frank Hill
The Clock House
Ivy yard.
Thos. yard, James
House

The Parsons B

HABUTS LANE

later
The Mall
School

The Minster

Dr Taylors

The Fox & Goose

Life
The
Chapel
on the
Green
1807

Jn Cant Bakehouse

Old Statut
& Mr J Gorman

OR
WAPPING

Nancy Butterfly
and the
The Quaker Shurds (Sheward)

The Tanhouse

Mr Packman's Cottage

The Stocks & Whipping Post

Jhn Callow & Jhn Tyler

Mr Peakman's house
& Ware Drawing Mill

Old Edward Jones
his Blacksmith shop

Mr Williams House his
Highest father Robert
Hill Esq. the Potter

Old Lord Ward a labourer was a lonely grinder

he was a labourer was a lonely grinder

Richard Stiles Farm

2 Houses still standing 1851

Old building owned Mr. Peakman
occupied Wm. Alcock & the Sunday Sch.

Quaker Shuard his house
Needle pointing mill
Chrisler Corle & Grant Coley

The Fountain

The Old Quakers Meeting House

Old John Morton's

The 2 l
be t

Pool Place

BREDON

Baker Smith
afterwards
Ipsley Workhouse

Old
Jom Turner

To Studley

OLD 'OLD REDDITCH'

There exists in Redditch Library an account of the town as it was in 1776, described by a Primitive Methodist preacher by the name of Joseph Monk.

In the handwritten manuscript entitled *A State of the Buildings in Redditch in the Year of Our Lord 1776 From an Old Inhabitant by Memory* the spelling and grammar leaves a lot to be desired, but he takes us on a tour of the town as it then was. Starting at the Unicorn Hotel (now demolished) he turns south out of the town describing the houses up Mount

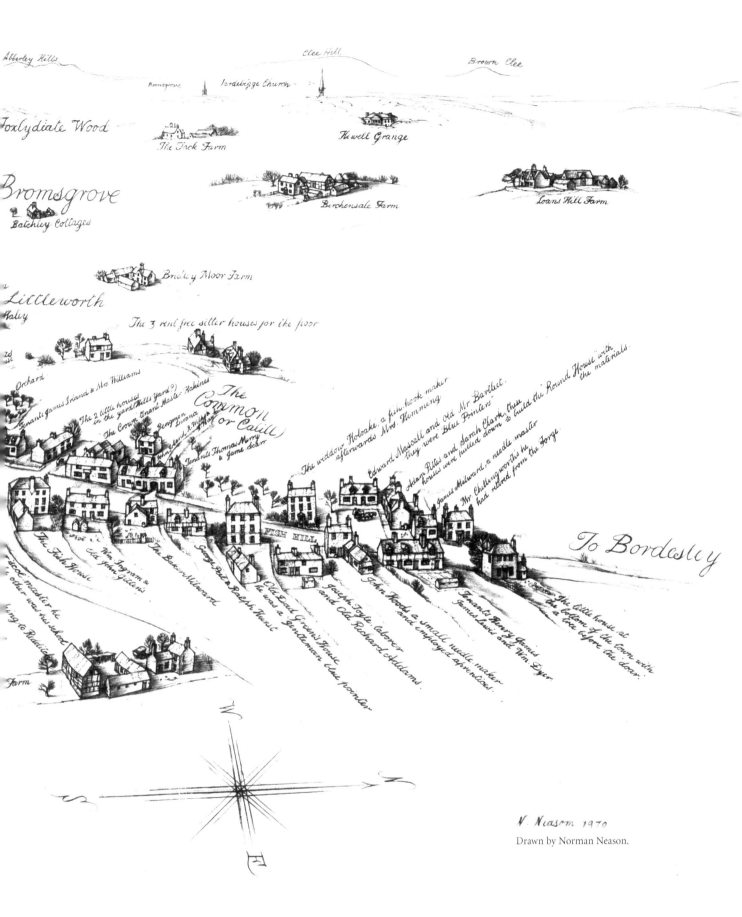

Abberley Hills
Clee Hill
Brown Clee
Bromsgrove
Isradrigge Church
Foxlydiate Wood
The Jack Farm
Huwell Grange
Bromsgrove
Batchley Cottages
Birchensale Farm
Loans Hill Farm
Bradley Moor Farm
Littleworth
Haley
The 3 rent free siller houses for the poor
Orchard
Tenants James Irland & Mrs Williams
The 2 little houses in the yard (Hills Yard?)
The Crown tenant Master Hakines
The Common or Calill
The widdow Hoboake a fish hook maker afterwards Mrs Hemming
Edward Moscall and Old Mr Bartlet they were Blue Painters
Adam Pillet and Sarah Clarke these houses were pulled down to build the Round House with the materials
Mr Chillingworth the had retired from the Forge
James Milward a needle master
To Bordesley
FISH HILL
The little house at the bottom of the town with a tree before the door
The Fish House
Wm Ingram & Old John Gillons
The Baker Milward
George Bell & Ralph Hurst
Old Lord Green's House he was a Gentleman Shoe pointer
Joseph Tytle Laborer and Old Richard Addams
John Woods a small needle maker and employed aprentices
Tenants Henry James James Lewis and Wm Dyer
Farm
V. Neasom 1970
Drawn by Norman Neason.

Pleasant as far as the 'wite heart'. He then returns to the town centre and turns right past the Fox and Goose (later the Royal Hotel) and on to Breedon (top of Beoley Road). He returns via the Fountain Inn (later Henry Milward's needle factory) and through the town to Fish Hill (Prospect Hill).

This description caught the imagination of local artist and historian Norman Neasom, who used it to draw up an illustrated map of the town based on the types of buildings known to exist in 1776.

An artistic reconstruction of Bordesley Abbey in the 14th century from the book of the Abbey by J.M. Woodward.

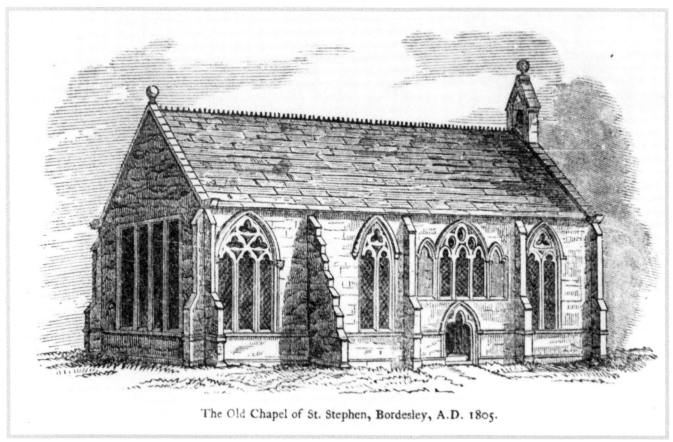

The Old Chapel of St. Stephen, Bordesley, A.D. 1805.

The old chapel at Bordesley Abbey, drawn by J.M. Woodward. It was demolished in 1805 and rebuilt in the town as the Chapel on The Green in 1806–07.

REDDITCH PAST~100 YEARS AGO~
(Copied by MR. J. M. WOODWARD, from an Old Drawing lately in the possession of Mr. Walter Guardner.)

1.—Dr. Hugh Taylor. 2.—The site of the old Malt Shovel. 3.—Tim Massiow. 4.—Perry's Blacksmith Shop. 5.—Johnson's property. 6.—The old Unicorn (John Mole). 7.—Butcher's Shop. 8.—Ivy House. 9.—New Chapel on Green. 10.—R. B. Guardner. 11.—Mrs Reading's shop. 12.—Richard Styles. 13.—Orchard. 14.—Scotch Fir.

This drawing by J.M. Woodward shows Chapel (later Church) Green in the early 1800s, shortly after the building of the Chapel, which was opened on Sunday 5 April 1807. It is a copy of an earlier drawing owned by Walter Guardner, who was from a family of local solicitors. In 1805 the Chapel at Bordesley Abbey, being in a ruinous state, was pulled down and an Act of Parliament for its rebuilding on The Green in Redditch was passed and received the Royal Assent on 27 June of that year.

Chapel on The Green, Redditch, consecrated in 1808. Much of the stone came from the old Chapel of St Stephen at Bordesley Abbey. On the left can be seen the Old Lock-Up on the corner of Red Lion Street. On the right is Evesham Street and the Malt Shovel Inn. The picture is an original watercolour after Woodward.

The Old Lock-Up at the junction of Red Lion Street and Alcester Street was built in 1824 and was in use as a prison until 1864. Immediately to its right is the White Lion Inn and the cone of the Malt House attached to the Red Lion Inn.

A lithographic print by Heming of the view of the town from the top of Fish (now Prospect) Hill in early Victorian times. W.T. Heming (born 1807) was a printer and the founding editor of the *Redditch Indicator* in 1859.

Redditch town centre, *c.*1800, looking from Market Place towards 'The Square' and the Unicorn pub.

Market Place and Evesham Street looking south about 1800. The Malt Shovel pub is on the left, and on the right is Perry's blacksmith's shop.

On the back of the original of this watercolour dating from about 1890 is written 'Old Tan House Back Hill & foredraught where bull baiting was held.' It must therefore show part of Ipsley Street.

Salter's Yard, Alcester Street, Redditch, demolished in 1912 to make way for the Palace Theatre.

This timber-framed cottage in Alcester Street, shown here being demolished in about 1905, was probably one of the last of its type left in the town. It could well have been built in the 1700s or earlier.

VICTORIAN REDDITCH

Rear view of 'The Castle', Crabbs Cross, Redditch. Built for (or by) J.M.Woodward.

J.M. Woodward, born in 1832, was a Victorian artist and intellectual who lived at 'The Castle', Crabbs Cross, from 1882 until his death in 1899. 'The Castle' still exists, a rather quirky house built to his own design. He was very active in the town, giving evening classes in art, English history and geography. His signature appears on several drawings and watercolours, but a good many similar pictures are unsigned and may be the work of his pupils.

Perhaps his greatest work is the magnificent book on *The History of Bordesley Abbey* published in 1866 at the request of local needle-master Robert S. Bartleet JP, who dedicated it to Baroness Windsor of Hewell Grange.

Most of the archaeology and all the book's content are the work of J.M. Woodward.

This satirical cartoon appeared in the *Redditch Indicator* in 1877 attacking members of the Local Board (forerunner of the Urban District Council), who objected to a scheme to provide sewers for the town. It was drawn by J.M. Woodward, urged on by the more progressive elements of the board who wanted the scheme adopted.

The victims went to court and obtained an order for all the offending copies of the paper to be withdrawn and destroyed, but one or two slipped through the net to remain for posterity.

Dr Herbert M. Page, medical officer of health to the Local Board, outside his house on Prospect Hill in the 1890s. It was Dr Page who, at a ceremony on 1 November 1899, deposited a 'Time Capsule' in the form of a glass jar under the foundation stone of what was then the new Technical School on the corner of Easemore Road and Archer Road. Later called Z Block, it was demolished in December 2005 and the jar recovered intact. It contained local newspapers, photographs, documents and other items.

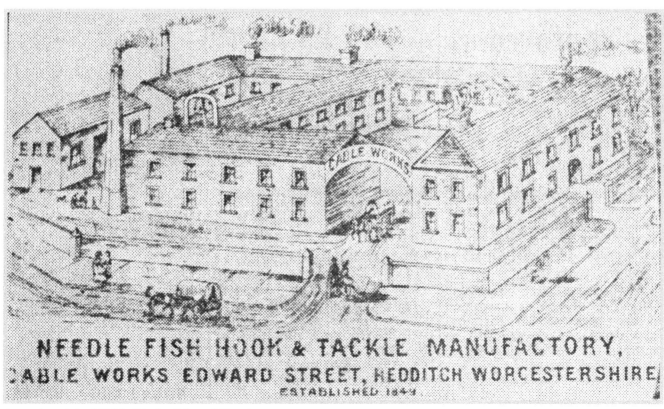

An early print of Cable Works, Edward Street.

The Literary and Scientific Institute, Church Road, later the town library. Erected at a cost of £2,700, it was opened in 1886 by Lord Windsor of Hewell.

Some of the Victorian inhabitants of Redditch taken by local photographers who were more interested in taking studio portraits than using the new medium of photography to record local events in the town. This was because of the long exposure times required in early photography.

MR. EDWIN SMALLWOOD.   MR. WILLIAM SMALLWOOD.

The Smallwood brothers, whose concern for the town and its inhabitants combined with their wealth ensured that Redditch's first public hospital and almshouses could be built.

The provision of a Cottage Hospital for Redditch was suggested as early as October 1865 in a letter to the *Redditch Indicator* by Mr William Avery, needlemaker, of Headless Cross, however nothing came of the idea. Several other offers of funds also failed to move the Local Board to action.

On 16 July 1892 a well-respected townsman Mr Edwin Smallwood died aged 83, and he left £75,000 made from the manufacture of golden-eyed needles. Among numerous other local charitable bequests was one of £5,000 'for building and endowing a Cottage Hospital in Redditch' and in addition a further £15,000 was given to Edwin's brother, William Smallwood of Alcester. A sum of £1,500 was used to purchase and demolish a group of dilapidated old cottages on Church Green West. Building work commenced in November 1893 and the hospital was opened by Lady Windsor of Hewell Grange on 25 May 1895. The fixtures and fittings were 'of the most modern type' and communication between all parts of the building was by telephone and electric bells.

William also gave £8,000 to establish Smallwood Almhouses.

Old cottages, Church Green West, now Smallwood Hospital.

The opening of the hospital in May 1895.

Smallwood Hospital, Redditch. Postcard view by E.A. Hodges.

A rear view of Smallwood Hospital in 1910 with one of its patients.

SMALLWOOD ALMSHOUSES, REDDITCH.

The Smallwood Almshouses at the junction of Marsden Road and Summer Street were built with a gift of £8,000 by William from his brother's estate. They were erected in 1896–97 and consisted of 10 houses with an Assembly Hall in the centre. They were opened on 22 June 1897, which was the day of Queen Victoria's Diamond Jubilee.

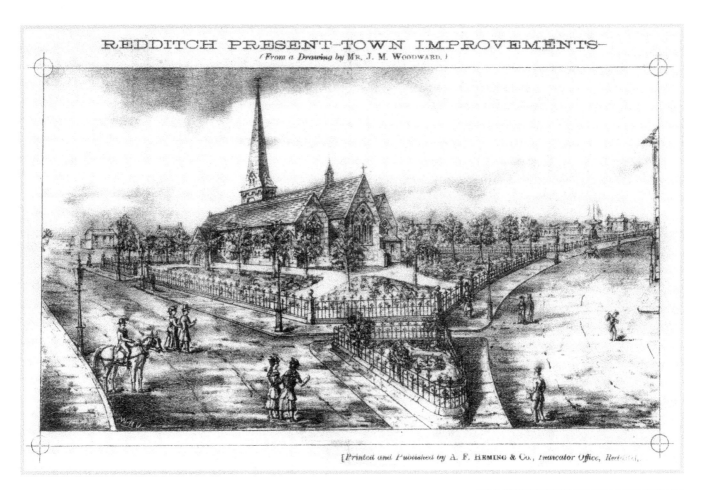

REDDITCH PRESENT TOWN IMPROVEMENTS
(From a Drawing by Mr. J. M. Woodward.)

[Printed and Published by A. F. HEMING & Co., Indicator Office, Redditch.]

ST STEPHEN'S CHURCH

When St Stephen's Church was built in the 1850s it was surrounded by a wall in close proximity to the church. This wall was demolished in 1880 and replaced by a low wall surmounted originally by iron railings (removed during World War Two). This plan drawn by J.M. Woodward shows that it not only surrounded the church but also enclosed the whole of the waste ground on either side of the church known as the Upper and Lower Greens. The whole area was then landscaped by a Mr Roe of Handsworth. Also improved was the kerbing and guttering of the footpaths and roads around The Green and plane trees were planted on Church Green West (The Parade or The Prom). The project was initiated by Mr Victor Milward. The committee included Lord Windsor who gave up the Manorial Rights over his portion of the land, and he performed the opening ceremony on 2 December 1880. During the day trees were planted by Mr G.W. Hastings MP, Mr R.S. Bartleet, Revd G.F. Fessey, Mr Victor Milward and Lord Windsor. The total cost of the enclosure scheme was £1,150, which was exclusive of £200 that had been promised by Mr R.S. Bartleet for the purpose of erecting a fountain at a later date. This was duly opened by Mrs Bartleet on 15 May 1883.

The poet 'Old Redditch', whoever he or she was, seems to be pointing out that the areas of The Green that were common land before the 'Enclosure' became Church land after the event. The 'Victor' mentioned in verse eight is a pun aimed at Victor Milward, chairman of the committee.

"THE CHURCH-YARD WALL."

Respectfully dedicated to the keeper of the keys of St. Stephen's Church-yard, Redditch.

The Church-Wall of St. Stephen's was seedy and old,
It looked so deserted and "Out in the Cold;"
And how could they manage to muster some Gold
   To build a new wall for St. Stephen's?

Apply to the Board! Its a pliable lot,
And try if the funds from the rates can be got;
They probably may not be down to the plot
   To get a new wall for St. Stephen's.

They applied for the wall, and they put their case well;
The Dissenters, however, had their tale to tell—
They complained in the press, and pronounced it "a sell"
   On the town for the sake of St. Stephen's.

The Church "They submitted" should buy its own wall,
There were places beside, do the same for them all;
Than go to the rates rather let the thing fall,
   What had rates got to do with St. Stephen's?

"Never heed," one winked silly, "T'will come to the same,"
And not to be banked in his 'Nice little game;'
We must call it 'Improvements,' and alter the name,
   We can keep it all right for St. Stephen's."

They got out some plans and propounded a scheme,
And "Church Green Improvements" was topic and theme;
That the wall was the object still none seemed to dream,
   The wall that surrounded St Stephen's.

A meeting at once 'twas resolved to convene,
And such unanimity never was seen;
They condemned the Church wall and the useless old green,
   But nobody mentioned St. Stephen's.

An active committee, with funds rolling in,
Decided most promptly the work to begin;
While the Victor looked on with a dignified grin,
   It was all going well for St. Stephen's.

They couldn't succeed, nor get at us at all,
By asking us plainly to build them a wall;
In the name of "Improvements" they've wall, green, and all,
   A very good thing for St. Stephen's.

The scheme too, on paper, looked "So very nice,"
"Wanted no competition," "They didn't mind price;"
And the rustic old green was cut off in a trice,
   And enclosed in the yard of St. Stephen's.

Shut out by that fencing, unsightly and tall,
Sufficient to cut off the view from us all;
We could see just as well through that seedy old wall,
   As the spikes now surrounding St. Stephen's.

In place of the Green that they've put out of sight,
Is a forrest of fencing that hides it all quite,
And a waterless fountain that wants putting right,
   Like the palings they've put round St. Stephen's.

Will the fountain and water turn out as they wish?
Will the Waterworks Company "Give them the dish?"
Or will there be plenty for Fountain and Fish,
   To play in the ground of St. Stephen's?

Let the Bells of St. Stephen's peal out in the blast,
Announcing the old Green a thing of the past,
And playfully tinkle, "We've got em at last,
   The Green and a Wall for St. Stephen's."

Nov. 25th, 1880.   "OLD REDDITCH"

Two photographs, one of Market Place and one of Church Green East, showing the church railings erected in 1880.

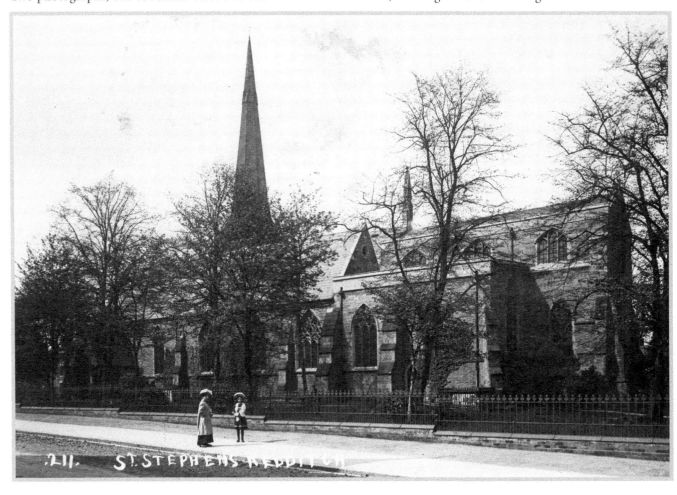

SOME VICTORIAN PHOTOGRAPHERS WORKING IN REDDITCH
The Graham brothers came from Halifax and were working in Alcester Street in the 1870s.

Thomas Hamblett came from Dudley and only stayed in the town from 1873 to 1875 and then moved on to Oldbury.

Richard Hodges was one of a family of hairdressers and photographers in Redditch and Astwood Bank from the 1860s onward.

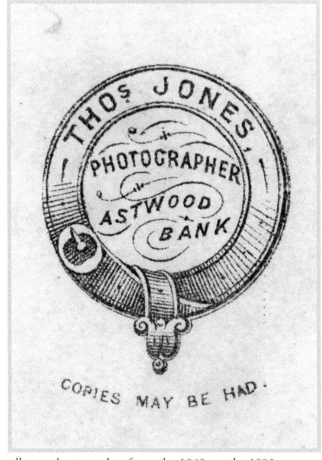

Thomas Jones of Castle Street, Astwood Bank, was a printer as well as a photographer from the 1860s to the 1890s.

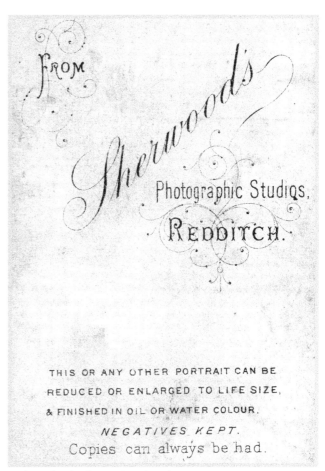

Sherwood's studio was at No.2 Alcester Street from 1879 to 1883. They also had premises in Chepstow.

Charles H. Evans' studio was at No.2 Alcester Street from 1884 to 1887.

THE EDWARDIAN ERA

Church Green on Coronation Day 1902. Flags are flying from the roof of the Bandstand, which appears to be thatched.

The elaborate entrance ticket printed by the *Redditch Indicator* Co. in the form of a postcard, which gave the holder entry to St Stephen's Church through the Porch Gate for the Coronation Day service on Saturday 9 August 1902.

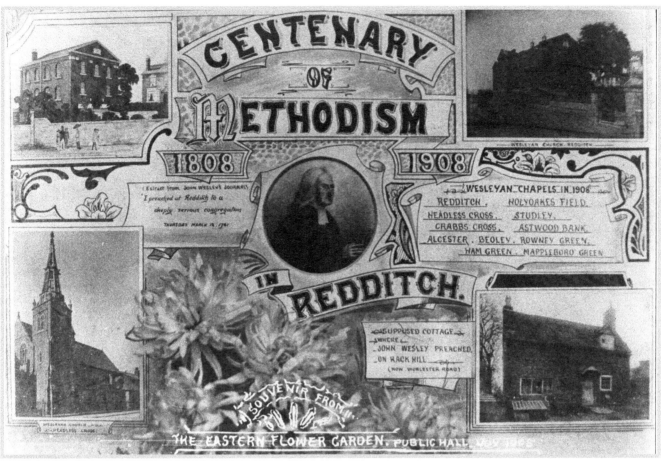

1908 souvenir card recording the Centenary of Methodism in Redditch. Also recording the fact that John Wesley preached here on 12 March 1761 at a cottage on Rack Hill – later Worcester Road, although other sources give different dates – on leaving the area he is reputed to have almost drowned crossing a flooded Beoley Brook.

Mount Carmel Roman Catholic Church in 1904.

Mount Carmel Harvest Festival in October 1906.

St Stephen's Church, *c.*1910.

Redditch Railway station. Note the advert on the wall on the right for James Thomas & Sons, Mill Street Needle Works. They were established in 1814, but the 1822 Directory gives them as grocers and general dealers. By 1841 they were making 'All kinds of sewing and machine needles, knitting pins, crochet hooks and every description of fancy needles, etc.'

This photograph of a new fire engine was taken from the railway bridge over Windsor Road on 25 October 1905. The 1906 *Redditch Directory* gave this description of the event: 'Trial of new steam fire engine near the Three Arch Bridge and on Church Green East. Trial in every way satisfactory. An invited company afterwards partook of refreshments at the Council House.'

Three Arch Bridge.

Church Road, *c*.1910. On the left is the
Ivy House and on the right is the
Institute – later the library.

Edwardian children pose for the camera on Church Green.

Church Avenue, sometimes Church Lane, is now just a path across Church Green. The view is from east to west.

An Edwardian view of the bottom of Alcester Street taken from Ipsley Green showing the old Liberal Club set back from the road, just left of centre.

A postcard by E.A. Hodges, stationer of No.1 Evesham Street, showing the speakers at a Liberal Party meeting at The Mount on 28 July 1906.

Two pictures of Chipperfield's visit to Redditch Fair in 1907.

A glass hip flask from the Plough and Harrow (now the Liberal Club). It was produced between 1906 and 1921 when T.H. Charman was the licensee.

Arthur Strain's cycle repair shop and general store at 38 Peakman Street in 1910.

This photograph of the old Plough and Harrow, which
later became the Liberal Club at the bottom of Mount
Pleasant, was taken in 1906 when Thomas Henry Charman
– the man in the doorway – had just taken over the licence.
He remained there until 1921 (when he died?) and his wife
took over.

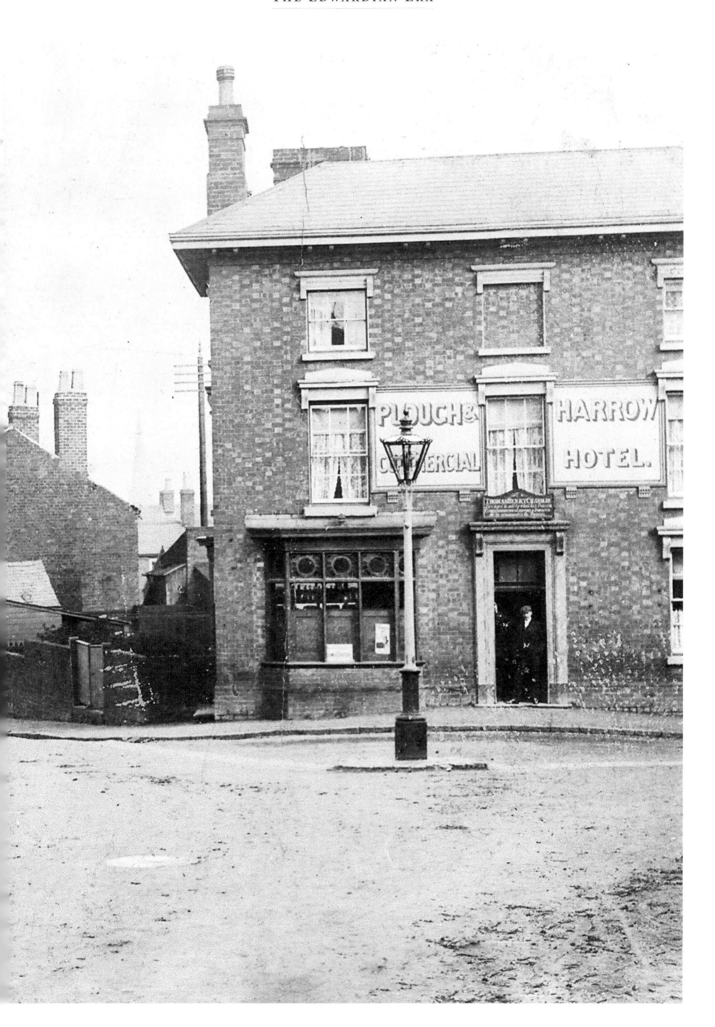

Front Hill in the 1960s, looking back towards the Plough and Harrow and the Black Horse.

The old King's Arms, Beoley Road, in the early 1900s, just before it was demolished and rebuilt in its present form. On the left is the Wagon and Horses, now no longer a pub.

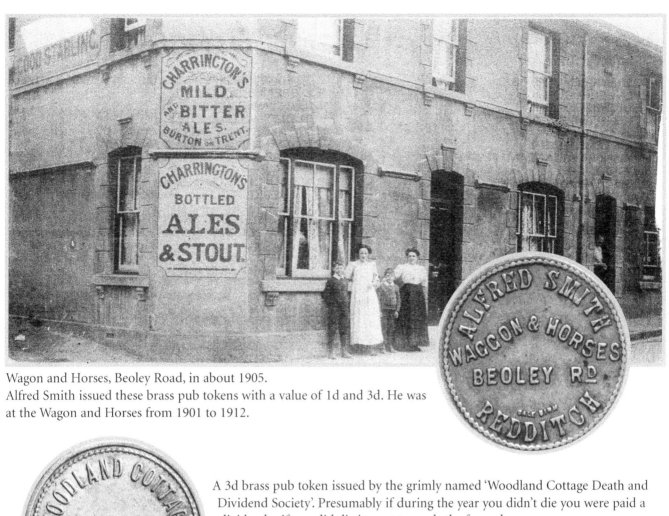

Wagon and Horses, Beoley Road, in about 1905.
Alfred Smith issued these brass pub tokens with a value of 1d and 3d. He was
at the Wagon and Horses from 1901 to 1912.

A 3d brass pub token issued by the grimly named 'Woodland Cottage Death and
Dividend Society'. Presumably if during the year you didn't die you were paid a
dividend – if you did die it went towards the funeral.

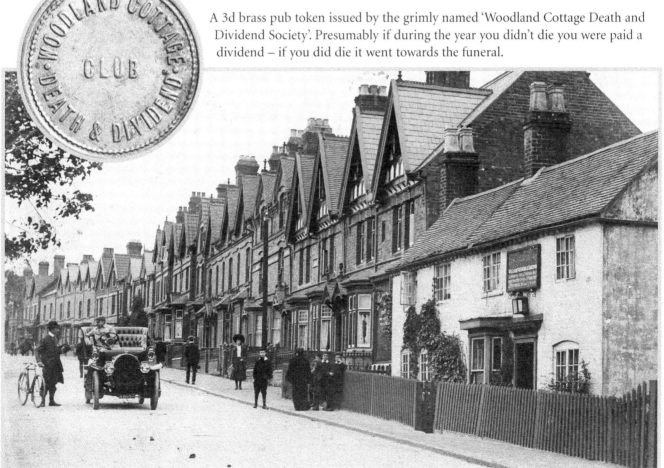

The Woodland Cottage in Mount Pleasant, photographed when the licensee was William Frederick Shelton. He was
there from 1905 to 1910.

LOCAL PHOTOGRAPHERS AND THE EDWARDIAN PICTURE POSTCARD BOOM

From 1 September 1894 the British Post Office relaxed the regulations governing postcards and allowed private firms to publish and sell picture postcards, but the boom in sending cards did not take off until it became possible to write the address and message on the same side. It must be remembered that the postal service in Edwarian times provided several collections and deliveries each day so that you could send a message to your friend across town on the morning and receive a reply in the afternoon.

Some of the more prolific local photographers who, in addition to their studio portrait work, took to the streets of Redditch to take what is now a wonderful record of images of Edwardian Redditch. Among the best were A.H. Clarke, Albert Green, L.L. Sealey, the Lewis brothers and Walter Terry.

A.H. CLARKE

The shop of W.T. Clarke at 47 Evesham Street sold cigarettes and tobacco as well as toys, games and cameras, and this may have sparked off A.H. Clarke's interest in photography. He ran the shop and a studio at the rear of the premises until the start of World War One.

An early Clarke's advert from the *Redditch Directory* for 1900, which may show Harold Clarke with his father.

Clarke's photographic studio at 47 Evesham Street.

Some of the excellent postcard views of Redditch and district taken by A.H. Clarke.

BEOLEY   CLARKES SERIES

Advert from the 1909 *Redditch Needle District Almanack and Trades Directory*. Now there was a manager to run the business.

CLARKES WINDSOR PORTRAIT GALLERIES 47, EVESHAM STREET REDDITCH.

HIGHEST CLASS
ARTISTIC & PICTORIAL
PHOTOGRAPHY
OF EVERY DESRIPTION.

EXPERTS IN
"AT HOMES"—AFTERNOON OR EVENING
BIRD AND ANIMAL STUDIES
CHILD PORTRAITURE
FANCY COSTUME EFFECTS
WEDDING GROUPS.

DAYLIGHT AND
ELECTRIC ARC STUDIOS.

Manager
VILLIERS ANDREWS
Silver Prize Medalist in Photography.

Clarke's advert in the 1911 *Directory* was in the form of a wax seal.

One of many of Clarke's photographs of the inside of Mount Carmel Church.

Another Clarke church interior – this one is St Leonard's, Beoley.

Two of Clarke's advertising cards, produced for local businesses.

Two cards taken by Clarke in the gardens at Hewell Grange.

One of a series of postcards sold by Clarke of Redditch Fair in 1906. He would have taken the photographs early in the day, printed them and they would be on sale at the fair by the afternoon.

2a, St. Georges Road,

Redditch,_____ 192

M_____

Memo from, **A. GREEN,**

PHOTOGRAPHER, & ·PICTURE FRAMER,

PHOTOGRAPHIC - ART - DEALER.

Albert Green's headed notepaper from the 1920s.

ALBERT GREEN

The initials A.G. or the name A. Green appear on many early Redditch 'Real Photograph' postcards.

He lived and worked from addresses in Grove Street and Birmingham Road but was probably only taking photographs as a hobby as his marriage certificate gives his employment as a 'fish hook filer' in June 1911.

His shop at 2a St George's Road sold groceries, china and earthenware in the 1920s and 30s and was presumably also a studio and darkroom.

Redditch photographer Albert Green's advert in the 1934 *Mount Carmel Catholic Year Book*.

: A. GREEN :

CHINA AND EARTHENWARE DEALER

GROCERIES OF EVERY DESCRIPTION

KEPT IN STOCK

PICTURE FRAMER

2ᴬ St. George's Road, Redditch

Redditch photographer Albert Green in a photograph taken near St George's Church in the mid-1950s.

This photograph taken around 1918 is of William Chatterley, Albert Green's brother-in-law.

Evesham Street.

Views of Evesham Street.

Front Hill, Evesham Street, showing the old Council Offices on the left – they were later rebuilt as commercial premises.

Two of the many photographic postcards produced by Albert Green of the Band of Hope Temperance March through the town in 1908.

This postcard showing Market Place, Redditch, in 1909, is signed A.G.

The top of Prospect Hill in 1906 with William Bartleet's 'Abbey Mills' needle factory on the left.

A postcard of Mount Plesent (*sic*) in 1910 by A.G.

A.G.'s photograph of the results of a fire at Beoley Mills, taken on 20 July 1906.

A Yucca plant in full flower on Church Green in 1906, long before the days of 'Global Warming.'

The old forge in Bentley Lane, Upper Bentley.

LEONARD LEYTON SEALEY

He was a semi-professional photographer and early motorcycle enthusiast. He worked for the BSA in Union Street (Lodge Road factory) and rode competitively for the Works team. In September 1919, on a 557cc BSA motorcycle, he took part in the A-CU's Six Day Trial and won a silver medal. He also won medals in the 1920 Scottish Six Day Trial and a Gold Medal in the A-CU's event in the same year. He and his darkroom moved several times as follows – Beoley Road 1910–12, 2 Other Road, 1913–16, 16 Other Road, 1917–19, 150 Other Road, 1920–23.

The BSA 'A' Team, winners of the Manufacturers' Trophy in the 1919 A-CU Six Day Trial. Redditch rider Leonard Sealey (centre) won silver and, like many photographers, appears not to like having his photograph taken.

A photograph showing L.L. Sealey's love of motorcycles.

This photograph of the Fox and Goose at Foxlydiate shows the licensee to be Herbert Fred Chambers, who was there from 1896 to 1922. L.L. Sealey's address on the back is Beoley Road, so the date is about 1911. The pony and trap belonged to Alfred Field, who was a chimney sweep from 56 Birchfield Road, Headless Cross. Note the mounting and dismounting steps on the extreme right.

Two football team photographs by Sealey, the Redditch Secondary School Old Boys and the Heath Spring and Notion Company team from Headless Cross.

Two Studley photographs of Sealey's – he probably got there on his motorcycle.

Two photographs by L.L. Sealey – Ipsley Green and Beoley Post Office – both taken about 1910 when he was working from Beoley Road.

Archer Road, Redditch, on a postcard produced by part-time photographer L.L. Sealey in 1905.

LEWIS BROTHERS

Their studio was at 2 Alcester Street, and they were in business there from 1894 to 1911. They had other branches at Castle Street, Astwood Bank (Wednesdays only 1899) and High Street, Alcester (Wednesdays only in 1902–04).

After Lewis Brothers ceased trading, Mr Arthur D. Lewis became the librarian at the Literary and Scientific Institute in Church Road (the old Library). He must have maintained his interest in photography as he provided the postcard-sized photographs for the 1923 *Redditch and District Illustrated Business Review*.

The studio at No.2 Alcester Street was occupied as follows:

1876–78	Graham Brothers	Photographers
1879–82	Sherwood, J.	Photographers
1883	Sherwood, B.	Photographers
1884–87	Evans, Charles H.	Photographers
1888–90	Hill, R.S.	Photographers
1891	Whitehouse, H.J	Photographers
1892–93	Whitehouse, J.J.G.	Photographers
1894–1911	Lewis Brothers	Photographers
1912	Cameron, D	Photographers

By 1914 No.2 Alcester Street was W. Gorin's greengrocer shop.

The studio at No.2 Alcester Street.

This Lewis Brothers advert from 1900 suggests that they must have had a night shift. They occupied the studio at No.2 Alcester Street from 1894 to 1911.

LEWIS BROS.,

Photographers

AND

PICTURE FRAME MAKERS,

2, Alcester Street,

REDDITCH.

PHOTOGRAPHS

Taken ANY NIGHT . . . . . .
by the ELECTRIC LIGHT.

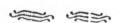

*Cheapest and Best Shop for
Picture Frames.*

Most of the photographic postcard views of the town produced by Lewis Bros. are anonymous, but all the portraits taken in their studio are identifiable. This card of the funeral of the Marquis of Hertford at Arrow in 1912 is unusual as their name is on the front.

Lewis Brothers 1906 advert.

LEWIS BROTHERS,
Photographers & Picture Frame Makers
2, ALCESTER STREET,
REDDITCH.

1906 SPECIALITIES.

MIDGET PHOTOGRAPHS from	...	3s. 6d. per doz.	
POST CARDS	... ...	2s. 6d.	,,
CARTES-DE-VISITE ...	... ...	4s.	,,
CABINETS ...	... ...	8s. 6d.	,,

Pictures of every description Framed in Best Style and at a Low Price.

PHOTOGRAPHS TAKEN ANY NIGHT BY THE ELECTRIC LIGHT.

An example of their cabinet-sized portrait photographs measuring 10cm x 16cm and costing 8/6d (42p) for 12.

Lewis Brothers' cartes-de-visite sized portrait, measuring 6cm x 10cm and costing 4/- (20p) for 12 in 1906.

An example of their midget photographs, measuring 3cm x 5cm and costing 3/6d (17p) for 12.

The price of this unusually large portrait measuring 16cm x 21cm is not recorded.

An early Lewis Bros. advert on the back
of one of their cabinet portraits.

WALTER TERRY

Walter Terry worked from Victoria Studios, 91 Evesham Street, (Front Hill) from 1904 to 1919. From about 1890 to 1900 he was a teacher at Wesleyan School, Ipsley Row. The *Redditch Directory* gives his home address as 'The Brambles', 218 Birchfield Road. He was a member of the Terry spring making family – his father was Alfred Terry, and he eventually joined the firm as a director.

The studio at 91 Evesham Street was occupied by several photographers as follows:

Harry Edward Coles	1897–1903
Walter Terry	1904–1919
William H. Fountain	1920–1933

Walter Terry's rather ornate advert from the 1907 *Needle District Almanack and Trades Directory.*

A greetings card produced by Terry and sent from Redditch to Weymouth in 1912. The card is from his 'Real Photograph Series'.

Redditch Congregational Sunday School pupils with Mr Fritz Heaphy.

More Congregational Sunday School pupils at their annual festival in 1915.

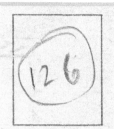

B. B. LONDON. SERIES Nº X. 90. PRINTED IN GERMANY.

POST CARD

FOR ADDRESS ONLY

126

A REMINDER.

That you may require for Christmas. Your Photograph as a dainty Xmas Card, prices from 2/6 per dozen. A Framed Enlargement in Black and White, Sepia or Colors. Private Greeting Christmas and New Year Cards from 1/9 per dozen. Ordinary Christmas and New Year Cards with choice wording. Your Pictures, Photographs, or Paintings suitably framed. Photograph Frames, Framed Pictures, etc., etc.

FOR THE BOYS.

Hobbies' Fretwork Outfits from 1/-, also Fretwood, Saws, etc. The New Strip work Outfits No. 1, 5/-, No. 2, 7/6. These Outfits make an ideal present for young people.

Your orders for any of the above will be appreciated by—

Walter Terry, PHOTOGRAPHER AND FRAME MAKER, **91 Evesham St.,**

(Opposite Council Offices),

TELEPHONE No. 65X. **REDDITCH.**

Walter Terry's photographic studio and shop also sold children's toys, as shown by this advertising postcard.

WALTER TERRY

Photographer & Art Dealer,

WILL BE PLEASED TO PRODUCE PLEASING PORTRAITS FOR YOU.

ANY STYLE.   RICH TONES.

ENLARGEMENTS IN COLORS, BLACK & WHITE OR SEPIA. OLD PHOTOGRAPHS COPIED.

91, Evesham St.

(Opposite Council Offices),

REDDITCH.

TEL. No. 65X.

ENGLISH GOLD FRAMES AND RE-GILDING. CIRCULAR AND OVAL FRAMES IN OAK OR GILT.

SPECIALLY EQUIPPED WORKS for the production of FRAMES suitable for Paintings, Photographs, Pictures, Drawings, etc., etc.

Reproductions of Old Masters and Modern Works can be supplied by

WALTER TERRY

Walter Terry's advert from the 1909 *Redditch Directory*, with no mention of children's toys.

All of Terry's adverts give his studio address as 91 Evesham Street, adding the information – 'Opposite Council Offices'. The postcard below, from 1910, shows the offices on the corner of Park Road and Front Hill. They were later replaced by Smokey Joe's Cafe and the Midland Red Club.

A photograph by Terry of an unknown chapel interior (presumably local) with its clergyman centre stage. The building was lit by some very elegant gas chandeliers.

Three group photographs taken by Terry at St Stephen's Girls School, Peakman Street, around 1918. It would appear to be a pageant for St George's Day.

The Headmistress at this time was Miss Alice Oakton.

AROUND THE TOWN

Evesham Street in 1905 on a postcard sent on Christmas Day of that year by Mr and Mrs A.D. Lewis. Arthur Lewis was one of the Lewis Brothers' photographers.

Evesham Street in about 1910 with Ladbury's well-stocked fruit, veg and game shop on the left. On the right is the Fountain Inn and its neighbour the Temperance Hotel. Two large, white-topped lamps in the distance mark the position of the Fleece Inn.

The grocery and provisions shop of Frederick Percival Dolphin at the top of Fish Hill – the old name for Prospect Hill.

F. P. DOLPHIN

FISH HILL HOUSE,

REDDITCH

FOR FIRST-CLASS . .

Groceries & Provisions

AT MODERATE PRICES.

Agent for Allsopp & Sons'

AND . . .

Anglo=Bavarian Ales & Stouts.

Hill. Evans & Co.'s Vinegar.

Grocer F.P. Dolphin's full-page advert in the 1912 *Redditch Needle District Almanack and Trades Directory.*

Old cottages on the corner of Church Road and Church Green West, which later became the site for the Redditch Benefit Building Society and then the Midshires Building Society.

A 1906 Temperance Festival at the junction of Church Green East and Alcester Street.

Bates Hill with the Wesleyan Methodist Church towering above it.

This postcard was sent to Wales in September 1906 by Charles Slater, who was the owner of Littleworth House (he spells it Lyttleworth). The house stood opposite the old railway station at the very bottom of Oakly Road, and the picture was taken from the entrance to the station. In the distance, on the left, someone is cleaning the windows of the Railway Hotel/Golden Cross. Higher up Unicorn Hill is the saddler's shop of J.T. Barrett. The cycle shop on the corner became Redditch Garages, and most of the foreground is now the bus station.

A close up of the Railway Hotel, 56 Unicorn Hill, now and previously the Golden Cross, with licensee Frederick Shelton standing in the doorway. He was there from 1906 to 1908.

Redditch Vicarage at the bottom of Plymouth Road.

St George's Church in 1904.

Pigeon's Bridge in Edwardian times, when this part of the Birmingham Road was called Clive Avenue.

A very peaceful Prospect Hill looking up towards the town centre from a point near Albert Street.

Two views of Hewell Road in 1906. None of the buildings have survived to the present day.

The whole of this 1907 scene of Ipsley Green is now occupied by Millsbro House, once the home of Terry's Springs.

Another view of Ipsley Green, this one taken in 1909. It shows the bottom of Alcester Street with the Primitive Methodist Church (now a bathroom emporium) just to the right of centre.

Two postcards showing an almost deserted Mount Pleasant. If taken today the motorcar would dominate the scene.

Four pictures of Redditch roads that still remain recognisable but are remarkable for their tranquility. They are all now dominated by traffic and parked cars.

A very rural looking Holloway Lane
just before World War One.

This 1914 scene of Mount Pleasant has changed. The tree has now gone and has been replaced by the road to the Mayfields estate.

The Cedars was built for Samuel Allcock in about 1880. It now provides residential care for the elderly.

AROUND THE DISTRICT

A very healthy looking Lodge Pool, now surrounded by housing development.

A leafy Lodge Farm in 1910.

Abbey Meadows flood defences in 1934.

A well-used footpath and bridge leading to Beoley Paper Mills.

The words 'Not Safe' are at the centre of this postcard view of Beoley Road Brook (the River Arrow).

December 7, 1901

People who use the Beoley Brook bridge frequently would do well to be careful for on the authority of Mr J Gross and Mr Perrins, surveyor, the bridge is completely rotten.

With the extra traffic, due to there being no bridge at Dagnell End for a while, it has been too much for its never great resistive powers.

Were it not for the danger to life and limb, we should welcome the news of its impending collapse.

For a moderate flood would probably sweep it away and then somebody, we assume, would have to provide a new bridge and that would be a reliable structure and suitable for the traffic it has to bear.

But in the meantime Redditch Council, with their usual lofty disregard of cost, are rushing headlong into the expense of a few nails and boards to meet temporary needs.

This article from the *Redditch Indicator* on 7 December 1901 shows that it was not just the river that was unsafe.

Muskett's Way through Pitcher Oak Wood connects Birchfield and Bromsgrove Roads. It gets its name from the nearby firing range, in use even before the Boer War.

Web Heath and District Flower Show, 1907.

A 1909 view of Lane House Farm, Love Lyne Lane, Hunt End.

Foxlydiate Stores and Post Office.

Two views of Foxlydiate Lane, now a busy access road to a recent housing development.

Two of the many postcards of the fete held in the grounds of Foxlydiate House in 1906 in aid of the NSPCC. The children's group were performing *The Pastoral Play*, and among the elegantly dressed ladies were Mrs Tarleton, Mrs Sutch and Mrs Hill.

The 'Meet' at Foxlydiate on 6 April 1908. The lady riding side-saddle in the foreground is Mrs Cheape, the 'Squire' of Bentley. Her daughter Katie is on her left, and the gentleman in the top hat is E.W. Haywood JP of 'The Sillins', Callow Hill.

Alfred and Ambrose Ireson ran the post office at 127 Evesham Road. The shop was also a newsagent, stationer and tobacconist. They published several postcards of Headless Cross, printed in Cheltenham by Burrows Ltd. From this view the pubs still exist, but the church is in danger of demolition.

Not a lot has changed in this scene except the traffic.

This view of Nailpasser Green, Headless Cross, dates from 1904 and shows, on the left, the Scale and Compass pub. It was demolished in the late 1950s. The Archers now occupies the site.

The shops in Evesham Road in 1904, with Mrs Daniels outside her greengrocery shop at 133 on the right. Slightly left of centre is the Forester's Arms pub – now a newsagent and general store.

St Luke's Church, Headless Cross, in 1905. Little changed except that the entrance gates are wider – again the influence of the motorcar.

Birchfield Road in the 1920s.

Feckenham Road in the 1950s.

Rectory Road, Headless Cross, now a dead end, except to pedestrians, after the construction of the Bromsgrove Highway cut it in two.

The old water tower at Headless Cross is still in existence, although its use has changed, but the needlemaker's cottages are long gone.

A Century of Trade in Redditch

Wellington Street and the Egyptian Foundry

The story of the Egyptian Foundry in Redditch begins in about 1840 when Mahomed Ali, the Pasha of Egypt, purchased steam hammers, to be used for pile driving on the banks of the Nile, from the Bridgewater Foundry in Manchester. He was so impressed with the machines that he asked that three Arab workmen be sent to England to train as engineers and return to Egypt to set up a factory there.

One of the three men was Affifi Lely, who was quick to learn and became a skilful engineer. On his return home after four years of training, he became frustrated with the slow pace of life in Egypt and at the first opportunity stowed away on a boat bound for England. He returned to the Manchester Foundry and asked for a job but was refused. He did, however, find employment in Birmingham at the Soho works of Boulton and Watt. At about this time he was involved in the construction of needle-making machinery for the Redditch firm of Samuel Thomas of British Mills, and he obviously liked the town as by 1851 he had started his own engineering works in Alcester Street.

His business succeeded after some minor setbacks, and in 1865 he opened his new works in Wellington Street (off Peakman Street) making 'every kind of needle machinery'. Also produced there were cast-iron kitchen ranges, water pumps, rain water pipes, sash window weights, boilers, cellar grating and many, many, everyday objects, including park railings.

In later years he was a familiar figure around the town, being 'of swarthy countenance, rendered more striking by his white whiskers'. He married twice and had a daughter, Ellen. He must have fallen ill in 1884 because St Stephen's Church Parish Magazine for 5 January 1885 records his baptism into the Christian faith and on 29 January records his burial.

A short time after his death the factory was taken over by Walter J. Llewellyn Ltd and was eventually demolished by the New Town Development in 1982.

Llewellyn's warehouse, Wellington Street, was originally Affifi Lely's 'Egyptian' Iron and Brass Foundry.

Llewellyn's warehouse, Wellington Street.

The full length of Wellington Street from Queen Street to Peakman Street. The plaque on the wall marks the entrance to Charles Greenhill's Enterprise (Spring) Works.

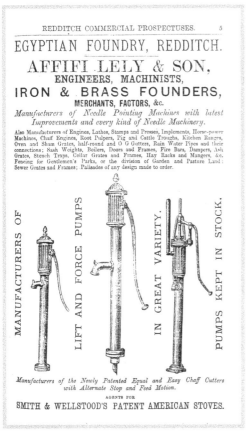

Advert from *Littlebury's Directory* of the County of Worcester 1873.

Advert from the *Redditch Needle District Almanack and Trades Directory* for 1879.

Smith Street looking towards Wellington Street. The yard on the right was used by Ada Herbert who delivered milk by horse and cart. The house belonged to Alfred Canning, blacksmith and wheelwright, and the building on the extreme right was his forge.

Top left of Wellington Street just before the junction with Peakman Street.

THE REDDITCH INDUSTRIAL CO-OPERATIVE SOCIETY

This Co-op Society was first registered in 1889 and was dissolved in 1900 when it was taken over by the Alcester Co-operative Society Ltd. The *Needle District Almanack* lists the Redditch Industrial Co-op as being in Headless Cross from 1892 to 1894, when the manager was F. Carson, who was later to become licensee of the Dog and Pheasant pub on Evesham Road from 1896 to 1899. Redditch Industrial Co-op Society issued this 2/- token. Other values probably exist but have not been found.

3d brass pub token issued by ex Co-op manager F. Carson.

The Alcester Co-op started in Alcester in 1875; by 1890 they had a store in Church Green East, and by 1894 they had opened shops in Alcester Street and Queen Street. The Astwood Bank branch of the Co-op opened in 1891, the same year as the branch in The Square in Feckenham. They later opened more branches all over Redditch but went into decline, closing them one by one with the advent of the New Town Development. This picture shows the sign over Branch No.9, which was situated on the corner of Beoley Road and Other Road.

An Alcester Co-op delivery van in about 1901. Note the lady's black armband mourning the death of Queen Victoria.

ALL HOUSE PURCHASERS should, in their own interests, immediately
BECOME MEMBERS OF A CO-OPERATIVE SOCIETY
The Stores of the

ALCESTER CO-OPERATIVE SOCIETY LTD.
are conveniently situated throughout the district.

Its Departments comprise Grocery and Provisions, Bread, Confectionery, Milk, Meat, Coal, Drapery, Ladies' and Childrens' Outfitting, Boots and Shoes, Mens' and Boys' Outfitting, Furnishing, Hardware, Crockery, Boot Repairing, Pharmacy and Optical, also Poultry Foods and Cattle Feeding Stuffs.

The Society supplies goods of first-class quality at
STRICTLY COMPETITIVE PRICES.

Daily deliveries of Bread, Flour, Confectionery
and Bottled Pasteurised Milk in all areas.

Coal delivered either in bags or loads.

JOIN THE CO-OP, AND LET YOUR DIVIDEND HELP PAY FOR YOUR HOUSE.

A 1933 Alcester Co-op advert.

Alcester Co-operative Industrial Society, Limited.

Received Share Pass Book No......1641......   July...10......1935

Total amount of Share Capital entered therein £ 20 : 3 : 9

Amount of Checks for Quarter ending July 2nd, 1935,
    including Balance from previous quarter   £ 20 : 0 : 9½

INSTRUCTIONS.—Compare at once the amount of Checks stated hereon with the total of checks for same period in your possession, and in case of any discrepancy send the checks, together with this receipt, to the Head Office not later than July 27th, 1935.
No Claims considered unless Receipts and Checks are sent.

Payment of Dividend and Interest.

When a member calls for pass book or withdraws dividend and interest on the stated days of payment this form must be presented.

No Pass Book will be handed out or dividend paid except on fulfilment of this condition.

The presentation of this form is (by rule) a complete indemnification of the Society against liability in case of payment to a person other than the member.

A 1935 Dividend Payment Form.

The Co-op tokens illustrated here were an early attempt at a discount system, but the metal coin type was quickly replaced by the cheaper and easier coupon system given with each purchase. They were collected in a booklet and redeemed at a later date – usually to help pay for the Christmas festivities. This token is for 2/- (10p).

Alcester Co-op dividend token for 10 shillings (50p).

One pound token (20 shillings).

This oval 10 shillings dividend token was issued by the Alcester Needlemaker's (N and M either side of 10/-), registered in 1888 and merged with the Alcester Co-op in 1909.

Alcester Co-op mugs from the 50th anniversary celebrations in 1925.

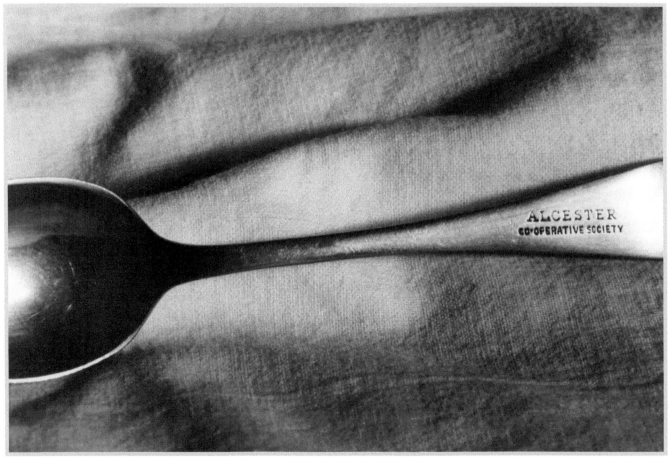

A spoon stamped Alcester Co-operative Society.

Embury Beck with his son Fred outside the shop at No.16 Alcester Street, just prior to World War One.

Old Friends are the Best.

So are old Boots when properly repaired. Do not throw away a comfortable pair of Boots or Shoes but have them skilfully repaired at

BECK'S, THE EXPERT BOOT REPAIRER, **16, Alcester St., Redditch**

Who has the best staff of Workmen and the most up-to-date machines in the District.

Beck's 1914 advert from the *Redditch Directory*.

Embury Beck outside his shop, which had moved by the 1920s to No.16 Church Green East.

A 1930s photograph of Embury Beck in his Salvation Army uniform with his second wife Harriet, whom he married when he was 80.

The Salvation Army premises in Ipsley Street (Back Hill) were opened in 1906. The Beck family were prominent members. Fred Beck, with white epaulettes, is at the front of this group taken at Easter in 1930.

Fred Beck, the bandmaster, with his euphonium, is sitting behind the drums. In later life he took over the family business, in the late 1930s, mostly working from premises at 209 Mount Pleasant.

A strongly-worded advert from Fred Beck, published in the *Redditch Indicator* on Friday 12 May 1967.

Ellis's cafe and confectioners was opened in the 1920s on the Parade (Church Green West) by Welshman Thomas Parry Ellis of Llandudno. It served the town until the mid 1950s. The person in William Street with the tray of cakes is believed to be Jessie Clews.

Ellis's advert in the 1936 *Redditch Needle District Almanack and Trades Directory*.

Another view of Ellis's cafe on the corner of William Street. Looking along the Parade, the next shop was Boyd's camera and photograph supplies, then the gas showrooms, the Birmingham Mail and Hepworth's.

In the 1950s a fire damaged the roof of the Ellis family home – 'Richdale', Birmingham Road, Bordesley, Redditch.

Redditch Carnival procession in Evesham Street and Market Place in the late 1920s, taken from the upstairs window of Ellis's cafe.

The Redditch Steam Laundry in Bromsgrove Road before the 80ft-high chimney was partly dismantled because of insurance problems.

THE REDDITCH STEAM LAUNDRY
Limited
BROMSGROVE ROAD, REDDITCH.
Tele : Redditch 347.

Name ....

Address ....

| | TO PAY | | |
| Mark | £ | s. | d. |

Van ....

THE FAMILY SERVICE
Finished Work

CONDITIONS

Name, address and list of articles to be entered on the other side of Label.

MINIMUM CHARGE 1/6

Articles not on printed list to be entered at bottom. Fancy Articles charged extra according to work.

Curtains, Blinds, etc. Every care is exercised in the washing of Lace, Muslin and Casement Curtains and Linen Blinds, but as they are so liable to become tender and frail by constant exposure to Sunlight, we cannot accept any responsibility respecting them. The same condition applies to articles with fugitive colours or fading.

COMPENSATION.—The Maximum allowed for lost or damaged articles is twenty times the amount charged for laundering.

TERMS — CASH ON DELIVERY

We would very much appreciate your recommendation.

In case of error or complaint this list MUST BE PRODUCED.

EXQUISITE DRY CLEANING
(Separate List provided).

PLEASE DO NOT KEEP THE CAR MAN WAITING

Redditch Laundry billing ticket.

6   *Advertisement.* 1927

Redditch Steam

Laundry

Bromsgrove Road,
REDDITCH,

FOR ...

QUALITY,

REGULARITY,

Moderate Charges.

Weekly Service to Redditch, Alcester, Studley,
Kings Norton, Alvechurch, &c.

A 1927 Directory advert.

Ferny Hill Brick Works showing its position relative to Bromsgrove Road, where houses are being built (1930s). Muskett's Way goes from the middle left to the top right of the picture.

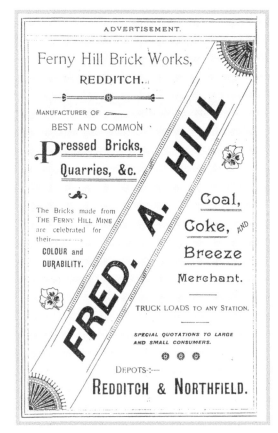

Fred Hill's advert from the *Redditch Directory* for 1900.

A pile of Fred Hill's bricks made at Ferny Hill Brick Works (FHBW).

A closer view of the brickworks showing the large round furnaces and smoke coming from the 130ft-high chimney, with the clay pits beyond.

Mr Hall – foreman of the brickworks.

Mr Hall and Mr Cox – top right with other workers.

Two views of the brickworks. One of the storage shed with piles of bricks ready to be sold and one of the chimney from ground level.

Holmwood is top right in this picture and Bromsgrove Road is top left.

Four warning blasts on a whistle marked the end of the brickworks chimney. It was demolished by Cater's, and it fell just where it was intended, between the two buildings on the left of the picture.

The 130ft brickworks chimney, built in 1929, was reduced to a pile of rubble in February 1964. Lowan's Hill farmhouse is just visible over the rooftops of Bromsgrove Road.

An original watercolour of Ricketts, grocer, adjoining the Unicorn Hotel in 'The Square', which was at the top of Unicorn Hill. It depicts the shop in 1794 but was almost certainly painted in 1894.

An original watercolour of Ricketts and the Unicorn Hotel after its rebuild in the 1880s. They are now also using the premises on the left of the picture, which had previously been a dwelling house.

A postcard showing Ricketts and the Unicorn. When the building was in this form, before 1880, it was known to all as 'The Cannister' because of its shape and the fact that it held tea.

William Ricketts, born in 1832 and died 1885.

Rebecca Ricketts (nee Welsbourne), born in 1832.

EIizabeth (Lizzie) Ricketts, born in 1867 and died in 1954.

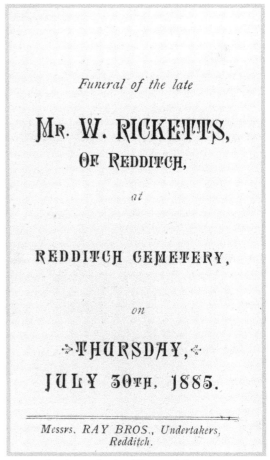

From the funeral of William Ricketts.

A postcard of Salters Lane sent as a Christmas card in December 1907 from the Browns in Redditch (owners of Redditch Brewery and later corn merchants in Evesham Street) to Mr and Mrs Grey in York (Lizzie Ricketts and her husband).

Albert Eadie in 1912.

ALBERT EADIE, THE CYCLE AND MOTORCYCLE PIONEER

Albert Eadie was a mainstay of the early cycle and motorcycle industry in the Redditch area and was involved in the beginnings of cycle making by the Royal Enfield and BSA companies. He was an inventor, engineer and shrewd businessman and a leading expert in transmission mechanisms. His patent Eadie Coaster Hub made a major contribution to the development of the bicycle in its modern form.

He was a Birmingham man, and before coming to Redditch he was works manager for H. Perry & Co. and also worked at James Cycles Ltd of Birmingham. He was recruited by the shareholders of the firm of George Townsend & Co. which at the time, in the 1880s, made small parts for sewing machines and cycles at their Givry Needle Works in Hunt End and was not prospering under the Townsend Brother leadership. Also recruited was Robert Walker Smith, who went on to become managing director of the Royal Enfield Cycle Co.

In 1892 Eadie and Smith took over the business and formed the Eadie Manufacturing Co., Eadie being managing director and R.W. Smith being works director. In 1893 the Enfield Cycle Co. was formed to sell the products of the Eadie factory, and both companies were still located in Hunt End. The 1896 *Redditch Directory* records the Albert Eadie Chain Co. Ltd, bicycle chain manufacturers at Hunt End.

Later, in 1896, the Eadie Manufacturing Co. relocated to a brand new factory in Union Street, Redditch, known to all as the Lodge Road factory. Eadie and Smith continued to operate as directors of both companies. The Eadie Chain Co. is also listed as moving to Lodge Road.

In 1905 Eadie's company was amalgamated with BSA Ltd, and he was given a seat on the board of the Birmingham company and retained responsibility for the Redditch factory but gave up his directorship of the Enfield Co. He took part in the design of many of the bicycle parts produced by BSA and took out a wide range of patents involving gears for bicycles.

He later became similarly involved in the design and production of BSA motorcycles until his retirement in the late 1920s. He died in 1931.

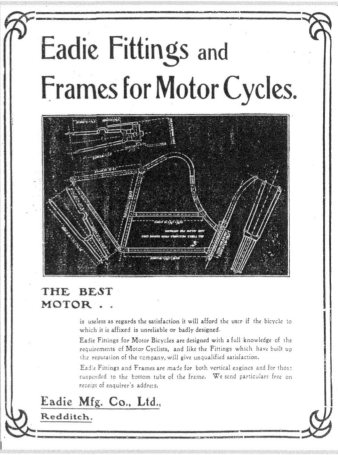

One of Eadie's adverts from an early motorcycle magazine.

Photographed in about 1930, this is the Britannia Batteries Lodge Road (Union Street) Works. The section of the factory in the foreground is the 1905 extension to the Eadie Manufacturing Co., built when BSA took over the company.

The gates to the main office block with the initials of the Eadie Manufacturing Co. and the date 1896. Although still in existence, they are now just a part of the fence around B&Q's warehouse which occupies the site.

The stone tablet, which was above the door of the main office block, with the entwined initials of the Eadie Manufacturing Company.

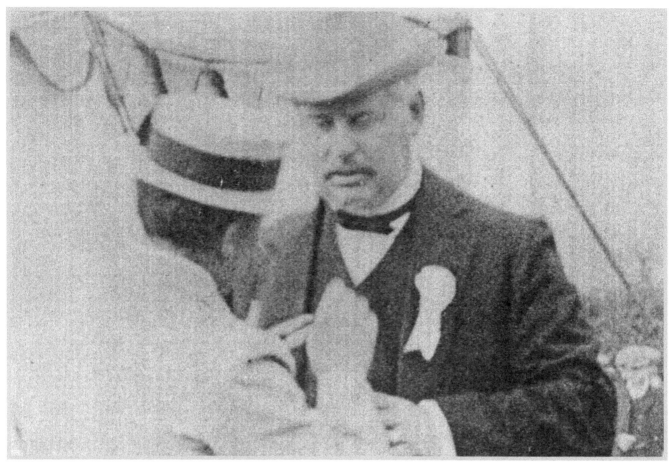

Albert Eadie at the 1907 Eadie Cycle Sports day.

Eadie Sports day 120-yard final in 1906.

Two postcards of the Eadie Sports day in Red Lane (Bromsgrove Road) on 20 July 1907.

Advert for the Eadie Coaster Hub dating from his time with BSA.

Eadie Mechanical and Literary Society stamp from volume 4 (January to June 1904) of *Page's Magazine* – 'an illustrated technical monthly dealing with the Engineering, Electrical, Shipbuilding, Iron and Steel, Mining and Allied Industries'. It was bound in book form by the Redditch Indicator Co. of Easemore Lane (later Road), Redditch.

An aerial view of the British Aluminium Company factory in Studley Road, Redditch, in the 1980s. The factory was originally Reynold's Light Alloys Ltd (Reynold's Tubes). It later became part of the T.I. (Tubes Investments) Group.

An artistic design made from sections of tubing showing the vast range of shapes and sizes made at the Studley Road factory.

Demonstrating the lightness of aluminium tubing on the works sports field in the 1960s.

REYNOLDS LIGHT ALLOYS
REDDITCH WORKS
Employees Early Pass 170

Check No. 002
Name
Date Issued 13/12/56
Time Leaving 5 Mins
Issued by G. Notley.

REYNOLDS T.I. ALUMINIUM LTD.
SPORTS AND SOCIAL CLUB
——
MEMBERSHIP CARD
1961

Member's Name ....

Reynold's Tubes Sports
and Social Club 1961
membership card and a
Works pass from 1956.

BRITISH ALUMINIUM CO. (REYNOLD'S TUBES), STUDLEY ROAD.

The Extrusion Press at the Redditch factory in the 1960s.

Welded tubing packaged ready to leave the factory.
The photograph was taken on 7 January 1960.

One of the 1,250-ton extrusion presses in the Studley Road
factory in 1964.

Drawing tube to size on a drawbench on 10 November 1964.

The off-line saw in what later became the polishing shop. Photographed on 16 March 1959.

British Aluminium managing director Tony Ponting with Margaret Thatcher when she visited the works in 1998.

Tony Ponting on the left with Margaret Thatcher and production manager Phil Glasspool.

THE 1920S AND 30S

Four pictures of Redditch in the 1920s. Redditch Garages are on the left with the railway station down the slope.

Redditch Benefit Building Society, Church Road, has been taken over and rebuilt.

A 1920s Unicorn Hill, now completely rebuilt.

The Queen's Head, Bromsgrove Road, is still there but the trees have all gone.

Church Green East in the 1920s.

The Fountain on Church Green surrounded by railings which were removed during World War Two. Note also the many plants in pots along the path; sadly, this practice would not be possible in the present day.

Two views of the town centre published by W.O. Parker. Walter Oliver Parker had worked for the Daimler Motor Co. and Enfield Cycle Co., but by 1920 he had a newsagency, tobacconist and confectionery shop at 51 Unicorn Hill and a 'High Class Coach Painting' business on Bates Hill.

The Cenotaph, Redditch.

Mr Ladbury outside his Alcester Street Garage with his son Douglas in about 1925. The garage was opposite the Palace Theatre, and it later became Huntley's Funeral Directors.

A very empty looking Birchensale Road on Batchley Estate with the gardens uniformly fenced off.

It would be wonderful if it were possible to return to quiet roads like these in and out of Redditch.

Rectory Road in the 1920s. In the distance, behind the lorry, is the Scale and Compass pub.

Not horses but motorcycles lining up for the Gymkhana held in Redditch in August 1925.

The visit of the Grand Master of the Independant Order of Odd Fellows (Manchester Unity) to Tardebigge Village Hall (now the Tardebigge pub) on 12 December 1925 to initiate the Earl of Plymouth into the Society. He also visited Odd Fellow's Lodges in Redditch.

A 3d token issued to members of the Earl of Plymouth Lodge of the Odd Fellows. There were many Lodges of the society in the area – this particular one was established in 1845 and met at the Fox and Goose (later the Royal Hotel).

The Royal Enfield Cycle Co. Fire Brigade in 1921.

The pupils and teachers of 'Tremorvah' private boarding and day school, Birchfield Road, in 1927. The Headmistress was Miss Symons.

Revd and Mrs Maddock in June 1931. He was a minister at Evesham Street Congregational Church. They lived at 'Elmsdale' in Hewell Road, now demolished and replaced by a chapel.

Salvation Army girls in the early 1930s.

Bridge Street (Holyoakesfield) school fete in 1930.

A photograph taken in the 1930s of Mr James Ames shop at No.4 Prospect Hill. The Central Cafe served 'Hot Dinners and Luncheons, Light Luncheons, Teas and Bovril.'

St Georges Road – the foreground up to the parked vehicles is now demolished.

Looking up Alcester Street on a market day in 1931.

Three views of Alcester Street in the 1930s. Cars are starting to appear.

The 'Select' cinema is on the left.

The view from Ipsley Green.

Mount Pleasant at its junction with Ivor Road.

THE PARADE, REDDITCH.

Market Place from the top of Alcester Street.

St Stephen's Church before World War Two. The 'gardens' in the foreground are the subterranean ladies and gents public toilets, now 'filled in'.

The top of Unicorn Hill in 1938.

Ipsley Street, at the corner of Red Lion Street.

REDDITCH. F.C. 1931-2.
PHOTO. JOE HARMAN.

Three 1930s photographs taken by local photographer Joe Harman, who began his career from 10 Evesham Road, Headless Cross, in 1911. By the 1930s he was working from 83 Lodge Road where his studio was a shed in the back garden, which was destroyed by one of several German bombs that fell in the area.

REDDITCH CHARITY BAND. 1933. PHOTO, JOE HARMAN REDDITCH

Cutting the first slice at the ox roast held in a field at the top of Easemore Road.

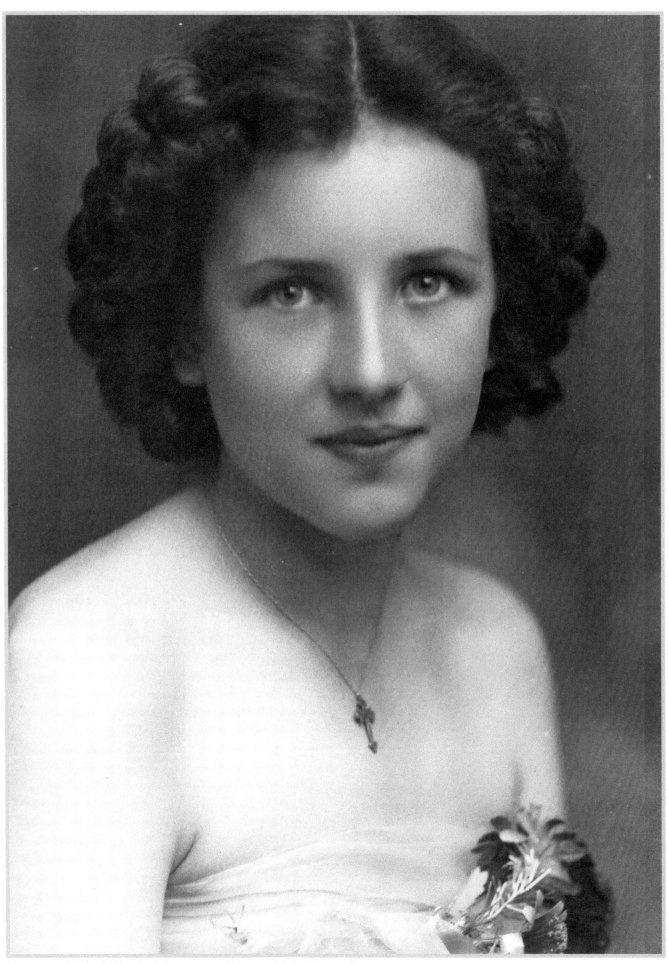

The 1938 Redditch Carnival Queen was 13-year-old Enid Mary Bowen.

The Fancy Dress group are waiting to join the Carnival Parade.

The Carnival photographs were all taken on Saturday 17 September 1938 by local photographer L.H. Boyd, who had a shop on Church Green West.

REDDITCH URBAN DISTRICT
COUNCIL ELECTION.

APRIL 2ND, 1928.

To the Electors of the Holloway Ward

LADIES AND GENTLEMEN,

For the past four years I have had the honour of being one of your Representatives on the local Council, during which time I have always endeavoured to safeguard your interests together with those of the town in general. Having lived in this Ward for eleven years I claim to have a special knowledge of its requirements.

I again offer my services for a further term, and, if re-elected, can assure you of my continued efforts in this direction.

It will always be my desire to **keep the rates as low as possible compatible with efficiency and service.**

The Council has many public improvements in view, but owing to local trade conditions is wisely deferring the carrying out of some of these much-needed Works.

I am at present a member of the Redditch Development Committee, which was recently inaugurated for the purpose of endeavouring to secure additional trade to the town, thereby, it is hoped, securing work for many, if not all, of our local unemployed. I need hardly assure you the Committee is fully alive to its responsibilities.

Should you have been satisfied with the services I have already rendered, I trust you will again give me your valued support on the day of the poll.

Believe me, Ladies and Gentlemen,

Yours faithfully,

GEORGE WHITE.

"Steepholm," Plymouth Road, Redditch.
March 21st, 1928.

Printed and Published by the Redditch Indicator Company, Limited, Easemore Road, Redditch.

1928 Election Poster.

Redditch Joint Burial Committee.

For the convenience of the Public, the Redditch Joint Burial Committee will undertake the Turfing of Graves and the Maintenance of same at the following charges :—

For Turfing - - 5s. 0d. per single space.
For Maintenance - 2s. 6d. ,, ,, ,,

Memorial Stones will be cleaned at actual cost. For particulars apply to the Sexton.

The Joint Committee are most anxious to make the Cemetery a Garden of Remembrance, and will be glad if visitors will deposit dead flowers in the containers provided or at the rear of the Cottage ; they are also requested to use the scrapers and brushes at the entrances, instead of using the grass borders and graves for cleaning their boots, and not to walk on the borders or graves. Paths under repair should not be used.

The Committee very much regret having had complaints of the unseemly conduct of youths, and others, when visiting the Cemetery, and they are determined to put a stop to same and ask for the assistance of the public in their efforts to do so. The Sexton has instructions to report to the Committee offenders so that an example can be made.

Dogs are not admitted to the Cemetery, even if accompanied by their owners, and any persons not observing this rule will be penalised by the Committee.

GEORGE W. HOBSON,
Clerk to the Committee.

Council House, Redditch,
12th February, 1930.

MOSES & SPOONER LTD., PRINTERS, REDDITCH.

1930 Burial Committee Poster.

Up to the New Town

Redditch Remembered

One remembers old Redditch in days of old,
many characters there were with stories so bold.
Remember the Mart and Friday night bidding,
three rabbits a 'bob', today you'd be kidding.

On steps of Select, Annie, Charlie and Cyril,
resting and talking, keeping Alcester Street's vigil.
One remembers them walking mile after mile,
always pushing their pram, crying out for some oil.

One remembers George Ramsey as we came home from school,
he just wandered around but was nobody's fool.
No betting shops then, no licensed bookie,
we went to Tom Johnson, to gambling no rookie.

Helped by Alf Hall to work out the bets,
five Skinners Building was quite a nest.
Tom was surely a man respected by all,
as straight as a die, and always on call.

And then, of course, was old Bertie Danks,
always around with good tempered pranks.
He'd stand on a table and show you his knees,
then he'd quietly ask for 'Half a pint please'.

The collectors we knew, each of their own style,
to get money in tin walked many a mile.
Remember Len Jarrett and Mary the Queen,
always tops as collectors, hard workers supreme.

Tip Harper's another who warrants a mention,
the years have rolled on, he's now drawing his pension.
Delivering papers for Dankie,and coupons for Waddie,
and making good friends with most everybody.

Gone are the days of the race for the train,
with bundles of papers, oh what a strain.
Grown men all running up Unicorn Hill,
in Summer the heat, in Winter the chill.

They sold Argus, Despatch and Mail all alike,
all carried by hand and sometimes by bike.
Saturday night the real race was on,
the better the runner, the sooner they'd gone.

First into the town meant a lot to those men,
sell all the 'earlies' and back down again.
Names like 'Pinnie' MacBeaman and another one 'Lap',
Arthur Danks on Church Green avoiding the flap.

Gone the Lamp, Alma, Plumber's, the Royal and the Fleece,
the George, Lamb and Flag and a quiet drink in peace.
They're all now demolished, seems ever so queer,
when for less than a 'tanner' you'd get smoke and beer.

The landlords were characters in their own way,
they'd allow you to drink and pay Saturday.
If you fancied a walk to King's Arms or Cricks,
you'd meet landlord Jack Hanson and Villa fanatics.

If the Villa had lost you'd keep your mouth closed,
if they won, all was rosy and no problems posed.
The same thing applied to the 'Lion' at Hunt End,
where to many a customer Jim Parry was friend.

They worked hard and played hard and oh they knew how,
if Villa kept winning, there was never a row.
The drinkers at home took jug to the 'Oak',
for fourpenny'th of porter, before days of Coke.

Red Lion street had 'Lions', both Red and White,
outside of both was many a fight.
A straightforward punch up, forgotten next day,
not like the present, a grudge till Doomsday.

The notorious 'Wapping' and Walford Street.
lots of people thought this, at least the elite.
They didn't know families who lived around there,
they were always dead straight and always fair.

Names like the Heaths, the Waltons, the Greens,
bringing up families on limited means.
In very small houses, up under 'The Arch'
and many took part in the 'Black Spot' march.

Bonaker's Pudding was famous around,
as well known as Wilson's and their Merry Go Round.
Supposed to have hairs on, at least I was told,
but I ate many slices, both luke warm and cold.

I could keep on writing, of this there's no doubt,
there's many more people I'm sure I've left out.
I apologise to anyone I should have included,
who think that they ought, but have been excluded.

Unknown Poet

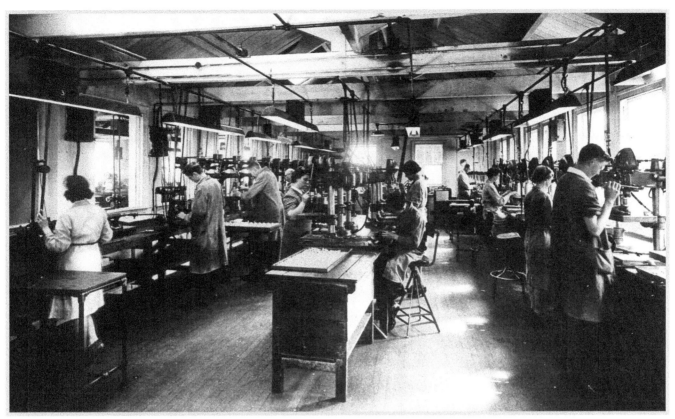

Inside the Mayfield Works of J. W. Young & Sons, normally makers of high-class fishing reels, but when this photo was taken in 1944 they were engaged in war work, which included making parts for Spitfire aeroplanes. The workforce pictured here are – left to right – Ethel Machin, Ronald Fletcher, Stan Gregory, Alf Locke, Dorothy Thompson, Dora Paice with Ray Saunders (seated), Lou Mountford, Mary Hollingsworth, Flo Coombes and John Rattue.

Redditch children in fancy dress for the VE Day celebrations. Back row – Scarecrow, Gypsy Pat Such, Ghost Diana White, Pierrot Betty Mogg, second Pierrot, Mrs Biggs (Elsie Siddele Downing), Mr Biggs. With headdress Sylvia Lewis, Gypsy Marlene (or Pauline) Hill, Sheila Maries Coal miner in front Colin White.

Elsie Siddele Downing

ADVANCED MEMBER: BRITISH BALLET ORGANISATION
(Ad. Teachers' Certificate) Ballerina British Ballet Company, 1938

MEMBER: IMPERIAL SOCIETY OF TEACHERS OF DANCING
(Teacher's and Artiste's Certificate, Highly Commended)

Member: INTERNATIONAL ASSOCIATION of TEACHERS of DANCING

Member: NATIONAL ASSOCIATION OF TEACHERS OF DANCING

ASSOCIATE OF THE GREEK DANCE ASSOCIATION

Principal of the

Redditch School *of* Stage Dancing

and producer of

The "Show of Shows" Productions

Training in all branches of the Art of the Dance
(over two hundred Examination Certificates
gained by Redditch Students and Pupils).
Ballet, Acrobatic, Tap, Rhythm, Musical
Comedy, Greek National, Ballroom, Eccentric,
Character, etc.

"The Dance is the Smile of the Limbs"

"LYNCOMBE HOUSE"

Telephone: 801

PARK ROAD   REDDITCH

Elsie Siddele Downing Dance School advert from the 1949 Redditch Carnival Magazine.

VE Day celebrations at Batchley estate in May 1945.

Redditch children performing *Robin Hood and Babes in the Wood* at Bates Hill chapel in the 1940s. They did a repeat performance at St Luke's, Headless Cross. Some of the children's names are – top left – Audrey Ralph Last but one Margaret Roberts – next row – 1. Margaret Davis, 2. Ann Wilmore, 5. Margaret Stanley (Maid Marion), 7. Brian Davis, 8. Roy Duggins, 9. David Wilmore Front row standing: 1. John Tongue, 2. Peter Bayliss, 3. Fred White, 6. Shirley Kilgalen. Seated: 5. Joan Griffiths, 6. Joan Duggins, 7. Cynthia Ralph, 8. Norman Stanley.

The Scouts' Gang Show at the Palace Theatre in about 1953.

F. Bennett and Sons grocer's shop at 40 Orchard Street in 1946.

Two night photographs of illuminations on Church Green, taken in the 1950s by local photographer L.H. Boyd, whose shop was across the road on Church Green West. It is not a winter scene as there are leaves on the trees.

Beoley Road in the bad winter of 1947.

The old Redditch Post Office in Church Road, which also housed the Manual Telephone Exchange. The Equipment Room, staffed by two engineers, shared the ground floor with the Post Office counter. The floor above housed 15 telephone switchboards of the cord and plug type and facilities for the operators. A new Automatic Telephone Exchange opened in Birmingham Road in the early 1960s.

Redditch Post Office Home Guard in 1942 at the rear of Church Road Post Office. Behind the group is the Manual Telephone Exchange equipment room.

Redditch Post Office cricket team in 1947 at the ground in Bromsgrove Road.

On Friday 20 May 1960 the Redditch Cricket, Hockey and Tennis Club sponsored a celebrity ball in aid of World Refugee Year at the Foxlydiate Hotel, Redditch. It was attended by several ATV stars, TV announcers and various minor celebrities, including blonde actress Jill Browne, Nurse Carole Young in *Emergency Ward 10*, and Roy Edwards, a popular singer from *Lunch Box*.

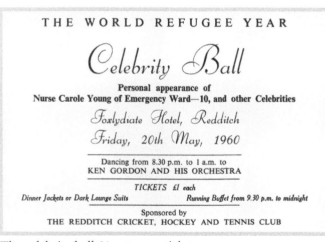

The celebrity ball £1 entrance ticket.

Jill Browne has a 'lucky dip'.

A good time was had by all.

Norman Hart's chemist at 125 Evesham Road, Headless Cross (now Spar grocers), and Lewis and Stroud radios and televisions at 129 (now an Indian Restaurant).

Redditch Market in September 1969 was on open ground quite close to its present site (not Market Place).

The top of Alcester Street in the 1960s.

The Plumber's Arms, Walford Street, just prior to demolition in the 1970s.

Looking down Walford Street past the Plumber's Arms to the back door of what was then Woolworths, now Tony's Handyman.

Bill Kings holding the Plumber's Arms darts club trophy. The pub ceiling was so low by the dart board that darts would bounce off it and still hit the board.

Pete Cassati ran George's Cafe (Smokey Joe's) in the 1960s. It was in Evesham Street on Front Hill on the corner of Park Road. After its demolition Pete's Cafe moved to Unicorn Hill.

Children in party mood outside George's Cafe in the 1950s.

Evesham Street (Front Hill) in the 1970s. The two shops on the left still exist, but the bus lane to the Bus Station replaced the Il Cadore Continental restaurant and shop on the right.

Evesham Street in the late 1960s. Below the Antique shop is the Il Cadore Continental restaurant, and next but one is John Dyson's electrical shop (No.116). Below that was Engineering Supplies Co., about four houses and a few shops including a barbers with Smokey Joe's cafe on the corner of Park Road. Just before the cafe was a doorway and stairs to the Midland Red Club on the first floor.

Another view of Walford Street in the 1960s with the caravans of Wilson's fun fair parked in their winter quarters on the right.

Striking Telephone Engineers at the Telephone Engineering Centre in Arthur Street, Redditch, in the early 1970s. They are, left to right, Ray Barras, Fred Wiggett, Dave Day, Bill Woolnough, John Rogers, Geoff Coley, Ron Evans, Neville Emms, Alan Evans, Doug Russell, Niel Shields, Alan Foxall, John Thomas, Bob Hitchcock, Alf Rogers, Arthur Walton, unknown, Brian Davies and Ken Raybould.

AND THE WALLS CAME TUMBLING DOWN

The Rose and Crown, Heathfield Road, Web Heath in 1926.

The Rose and Crown just prior to demolition in the 1970s.

Non-drinker Ernie Cater inside the Rose and Crown just before he demolished it. The pub was rebuilt and reopened in June 1978.

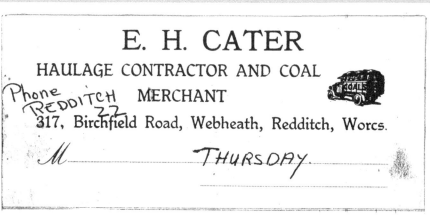

Examples of Ernie Cater's business stationery.

Ernie Cater's business stationery.

This photograph appeared in the *Redditch Indicator* in September 1956 and according to the report shows work in progress on the demolition of the old cottages behind the junction of Peakman Street and Archer Road. Redditch College of Further Education was later built on the site. However, Ernie Cater's photographic archive records it as the demolition of Smallwood Row on 14 September 1956.

On 11 August 1958 Harry Taylor, chairman of Redditch Council, struck the first blow in the demolition of part of Britten Street, watched by Ernie Cater and his workers.

Littleworth House stood opposite the old Railway Station at the very bottom of Oakly Road on the site now occupied by the bus station. At the time of its demolition in March 1960 it was being used as the offices of the Ministry of Pensions and National Insurance.

Pitt's (Redditch) Ltd Motor Engineers had showrooms in Evesham Street, but the service department was at the top of Park Road at the back of Smokey Joe's cafe. The photograph, taken in January 1961, shows the Cater team's equipment preparing to clear the site which became John Bryant & Son's Garage.

Pitt's Garage advert from the 1948 Redditch Carnival Magazine.

The Cater team at work in George Street in March 1965.

The demolition of Abbey Mills, Prospect Hill. It was originally William Bartleet's needle and fish hook factory. Clarke's Springs Ltd built a new factory on the site (Sinew Works), which was in turn demolished a few years later to make way for Grosvenor House.

The demolition of properties in Red Lion Street in about 1970. The Warwick Arms pub in Ipsley Street can be seen top centre.

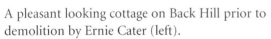

Ernie Cater and his men demolishing houses at the top of Ipsley Street in the late 1950s.

A pleasant looking cottage on Back Hill prior to demolition by Ernie Cater (left).

The view down Ipsley Street (Back Hill) in the 1950s, before the area was cleared for redevelopment.

The view down Ipsley Street in the 1970s. The Salvation Army building remains on the right, but where the white car is parked in the centre there is now a bus lane to the bus station.

Sport

The 1905 members of Dixon's Athletic Football Club may well be from Tardebigge.

The 1906–07 team of Redditch Athletic football club.

St Stephen's Junior football team 1954–55 season.

Skaters on Lodge Pool in February 1907.

Hewell Road swimming baths were still alfresco in August 1908.

Redditch Rovers Reserves had a second team seen here in the 1909–10 season.

St George's Church Juniors football team pose for a photograph taken in 1911 by L.L. Sealey who lived nearby.

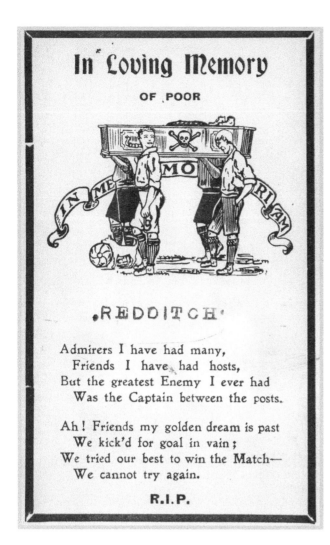

In Loving Memory

OF POOR

.REDDITCH.

Admirers I have had many,
    Friends I have had hosts,
But the greatest Enemy I ever had
    Was the Captain between the posts.

Ah! Friends my golden dream is past
    We kick'd for goal in vain;
We tried our best to win the Match—
    We cannot try again.

R.I.P.

Redditch Physical Culture Club at the Territorial Army Barracks, Easemore Road. The club was run by Harry Harris, fourth from the right on the front row.

A card sent 'From Will' after a match against a Redditch football team.

The winners of the Redditch and District schoolboy's relay in 1931.

The Rifleman (pub, bottom of Park Road) Air Gun Club who won the Redditch League Cup in 1927.

Feckenham Rovers football team pictured in the 1934–35 season. Back row: Percy Chatterley, George Owen, Ernie Kings, Albert Prescott, Frank Slade, Norman 'Noddy' Ralph, Fred Morris, Tom Archer, Bern Slade, Joseph Ralph, Albert Bradley. Middle row: Arthur Davis, Bill Brookes, Norman Smith, Harry Padghem, Bill Betteridge, Wally Ledbury, Eric Halliband, Charles Bayliss. Front row: (Boys) Denis Bayliss, Jake Slade.

The second team of St Peter's Church, Ipsley Juniors football club in the 1940s.

In 1971 Redditch United reached the first round of the FA Cup. On Saturday 20 November at the Valley Stadium, Redditch, they held Peterborough United to a 1–1 draw. There was a replay on the Monday evening which they lost. The team was: Les Brooks, Trevor Rees, Mick Evans, Dave Owen, Paul Rock, Mick Guise, Nick Ingram, Alan Walker, Ray Howell, Doug Pash, David Gilbert, Brian Smart (sub).

CRABBS CROSS, ASTWOOD BANK AND FECKENHAM

The original Fleece Inn, Crabbs Cross, began life as a row of cottages. The end one was a butcher's shop run by Fred Chambers who, in 1872, took over the beer house next door. He eventually merged the two premises and concentrated on being a pub landlord.

The Fleece Inn was rebuilt in 1897.

The chip shop and the buildings on the left side of Evesham Road remain almost intact but all on the right side have now gone.

One of the many ox roasts held at the Red Lion, Hunt End. This one appears to be in the 1920s.

There are now more houses in the centre of the picture and Enfield Road has been a cul-de-sac since the construction of Windmill Drive.

A token for 1d issued by the Enfield Club in 1905.

The Royal Enfield Club, Crabbs Cross, in 1905. In 1914 it became Treadgold's Picture House until about 1930. More recently it was Latham's Brush factory and is now being renovated and will become flats.

The picture shows Lady Georgina Vernon spreading the mortar for the foundation stone of the extension to the church of St Matthias and St George in Church Road, Astwood Bank, on Whit Tuesday in 1911. The extension which doubled the size of the church was built by the local firm of George Huxley.

A religious service at Astwood Bank was part of the 1911 Coronation celebrations on 22 June. The postcard was sent to a friend in London by someone who was 'by the flag'.

Chapel Street, Astwood Bank, in 1905.

A church treat in Astwood Bank in 1908 with 'Britannia' wearing a fireman's helmet on the horse-drawn wagon.

Evesham Road, Astwood Bank.

A gathering that would be highly dangerous in the present
day at this busy crossroads.

Astwood Bank Adult
School enamel badge.

The Astwood Bank Adult School Sports day in July 1907 appears to have been supported by all the village children.

George Hollington & Son's needle factory (St Crispin Works), Church Road, in the 1950s. Behind the van in the distance is the Red Lion Inn.

This engraving of Perkins and Son's needle factory in Astwood Bank appeared in the *Illustrated Midland News* on 19 February 1870. An accompanying article gave details of their output: they produced over 500 gross of needles per week and employed 120 men, women, boys and girls.

The Pound House at the bottom of The Square, Feckenham. The pound for stray livestock is on the right.

The old Feckenham couple pictured here are thought to be from the Davis family. In 1879 (about the time of the photograph) Arthur Davis was a farmer, builder and also a carrier, travelling to Bromsgrove on Tuesdays and Birmingham on Thursdays.

The Lygon Arms in 1909, when Frederick J. Sprosen was licensee. Mrs Sprosen can be seen in the pub doorway.

Feckenham Court Leet procession on 29 June 1913.

Noah's Green on the Saltway to Droitwich.

The old mill.

Feckenham blacksmith George Newman with his son Peter.

This, the first of five views of Feckenham High Street, shows the Eight Bells pub on the left.

This postcard was published by A.G. Baker, whose shop is on the left. He was a grocer and corn dealer and kept the post office. It is notable that he also sold buckets and shovels.

Village children posing for the camera in 1905.

More children posing outside Feckenham House in 1909.

One of several shops that flourished in the High Street in 1913.

Ipsley, Beoley and Bordesley

Ipsley Court, one-time home of Walter Savage Landor, was saved from the bulldozers when it became the offices for the Law Society.

St Peter's Church with Ipsley Court in the background in 1931.

A young man trying his luck in the River Arrow in 1905.

Nothing is known about this enterprise as it does not appear in any trade directory.

Washford Mill, once a needle mill, now a pub. It is reputed to be the mill at Ipsley mentioned in the *Domesday Book*.

Another mill at Ipsley – the large building on the right is Ipsley Mill. It no longer exists but the mill cottages remain. In the 1880s William Gale was using water power here and at Beoley Mills for needle and fish hook scouring.

By the late 1890s the Hunt brothers were using it for the same purpose, but by 1905 it was being used by Miss Hill to teach dressmaking and fancy needlework. This advert is from the *Redditch Needle District Almanack and Trades Directory*.

Beoley Church and Vicarage in 1904, which is not so visible these days due to 100 years of tree growth.

Beoley Hall, once a private residence, is now converted into apartments.

Beoley Road Brook – the River Arrow – was a dangerous place when flooded.

The problem was solved by a new bridge shown here on a card posted to London in August 1934.

Redditch. Holt End, Beoley

The cottages at Holt End looking towards Redditch.

A very unusual, octagonal 3d brass pub token issued by one of the Whitmore family who were licensees from 1872 to 1890.

Looking the other way gives a view of Holt Hill and the Village Inn.

Originally a forge, the tea rooms were run by
Mrs Reynolds and her three daughters and
were popular with cyclists until World War
Two. It is now a private residence.

Beoley Village in 1904. A
sign on the shop advertises
W.E. Smith's mineral water.

Beoley Garage, Branson's Cross, in the 1950s –
the crossroads is now replaced by an underpass
on a very busy dual carriageway.

Bordesley Lodge Farm in the 1920s.

Bordesley Hall was the home, for many years, of the Cast Iron Research Association. Seen here on a card sent to Paris in 1910, it is now known as the Castings Development Centre.

Bentley, Hewell and Tardebigge

Bentley Manor, Upper Bentley, near Redditch on a card bearing the old Redditch town crest posted in 1906. The house was demolished in 1955.

A medal produced for Mrs Cheape, the 'Squire' of Bentley, and presented by her to her staff on the occasion of Queen Victoria's Jubilee.

The billiard room reflects the 'hunting, shooting and fishing' lifestyle of the various Squires of Bentley.

The family, friends and estate workers gathered in front of the main entrance to Bentley Manor on the occasion of Hugh Annesley Cheape's 21st birthday on 15 November 1899. Hugh is seated centre, on his right is his mother, 'the Squire', and on his left is his sister Maude – later Maude Ellis, who wrote her family's history in the book *The Squire of Bentley*. Underneath the photograph is written, possibly by Hugh himself, 'With Mr Hugh Annesley Cheape's Compliments November 15th 1899.'

The main gates of Bentley Manor in its heyday in the Edwardian era.

Original railings at Bentley Manor's old main entrance, photographed in 1998.

Where the house once looked out across Worcestershire to the Malvern Hills, now a forestry plantation.

The pack of hunting dogs owned by Mrs Cheape, photographed by the pond at the bottom of the 'Army Field' below the manor house in 1906.

This picture of the ford and footbridge in Pumphouse Lane is entitled 'Bentley Brook', but the stream is actually called Swan's Brook. It was taken in 1907 by Bromsgrove photographer W. Daniel.

The appropriately named 'Ivy Cottage' in Lower Bentley.

The Hewell Estate was part of the land owned by the Cistercians of Bordesley Abbey. It was supposedly forced on the Windsor family against their wishes in exchange for their estates in Stanwell by Henry VIII in 1542, after the Dissolution of the Monasteries. Hewell Old Hall was built in the 1700s on land near a lake, but by the 1880s it was in a poor state of repair and its foundations were sinking. Princess (later Queen) Victoria visited it on 6 November 1832.

HEWELL GRANGE *The ... Seat of the Right Honourable Baron Windsor of Stanwell. Erected in the years 1884 to 1891.*

The new hall took several years to build, with a labour force of 130 men. The 3ft thick walls are of red sandstone bought by canal from Runcorn in Cheshire as the local sandstone was not of suitable quality (although, in 1853, it was thought good enough by the then Earl of Plymouth to build St Stephen's Church, Redditch. This resulted in the townsfolk having to bear the cost of regular restoration). The interior walls are of brick made locally at the Tardebigge Brick and Pottery Works on the nearby canal. Even these interior walls are over 2ft thick.

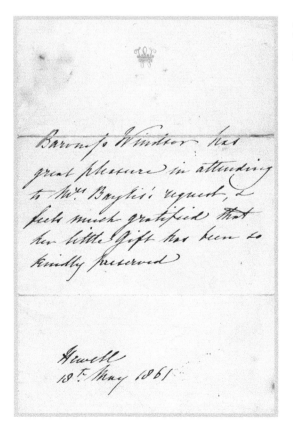

A letter on Hewell Estate notepaper from Baroness Windsor in 1861. This would be from the old hall which is now just a picturesque ruin.

SAMUEL FRISBY,

TARDEBIGGE, BROMSGROVE,

Brick and Pottery Works,

MANUFACTURER OF ALL KINDS OF

BRICK QUARRIES (9in. AND 6in.) PRESSED BRICKS,

Moulded Bricks, various patterns;

RUSTIC TREE POTS, VARIOUS DESIGNS.

FLOWER POTS AND STANDS,

DRAIN PIPES.

Rhubarb and Sea Kale Covers, Seed Pans—Round and Square.

Chimney Pots, Flower Vases and Stands, Washing Pans, Milk Pans, Cream Steins, Butter Pots, in White, Brown and Black Glazeware.

GARDEN EDGING, RIDGE TILES AND ROOFING TILES.

Prices on Application.   Orders Promptly Executed.

Tardebigge Brickworks advert in the 1900 *Bromsgrove Directory*.

The gardens at Hewell with their topiary, lawns and fountains would have needed a large staff of gardeners to maintain them. It is not a problem in the present day as the hall is now a Borstal Institution.

The stone door to a grotto in the gardens at Hewell in about 1910.

The indoor tennis courts at Hewell are in a separate building some way from the main house, now used as a gymnasium.

A card posted in June 1911 showing the 'Grass Terrace' in Hewell gardens, which leads up to the water tower, and still exists close to the old Redditch to Bromsgrove road.

A cigarette card of Hewell Grange, which was issued in 1923 in a packet of Player's cigarettes. Thus, collectors of the cards were encouraged to buy and smoke more cigarettes.

On the occasion of the coming of age of the Hon. Other Robert Windsor-Clive in 1905, medals were struck in bronze and white metal and presented to the children of estate workers.

A sketch of the earl from the *Redditch Needle District Almanack and Trades Directory*.

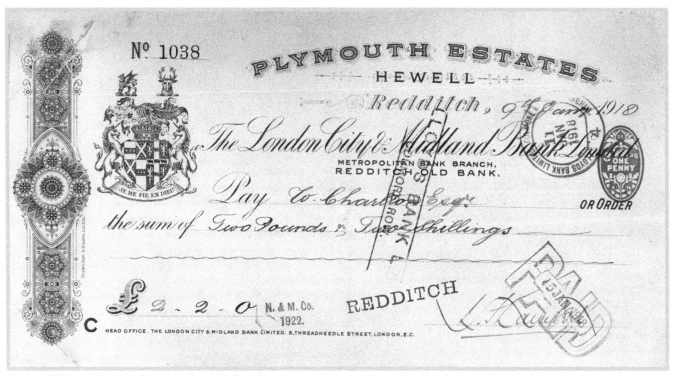

A Hewell Estate cheque for £2 2s (£2.10) dated January 1918, payable to W. Charlton of the Deaf and Dumb Institution. It was signed by Lionel Foley Lambert JP of Greenhill House. He was agent to the Earl of Plymouth from approximately 1910 to 1934. He was also vice-president of Hewell Cricket Club and served on many other local committees.

An ivy-clad Tardebigge Church in 1907 and the scaffolding-clad church tower during restoration in October 1993.

The vicar of Tardebigge, the Revd C.A. Dickens MA. Hon. Canon of Worcester and his wife. Their daughter Margaret wrote a history of the parish published in 1930 entitled *A Thousand Years in Tardebigge*.

The book *A Thousand Years in Tardebigge* records the fact that Dusthouse Farm was in existence as far back as 1514, when it was called 'Piplars'. When this picture was taken in 1908 it was owned and farmed by John Taylor.

These two photographs of the north and south ends of Tardebigge canal tunnel are prime candidates for the 'Most Boring Postcard' competition.

The Tardebigge canal, drained for repairs in January 1996. The 'Cressy' Memorial is centre right.

The polished brass medal produced by the Worcester and Birmingham Canal Society in 1981 to mark the unveiling of the 'Cressy' Memorial. The Memorial plaque on its plinth is on the far side of the Top Lock.

An apple box dated 1960.

The offices of Tardebigge Orchards Ltd at Broad Green in July 1970.

STUDLEY, MAPPLEBOROUGH
AND GORCOTT

Workers outside the Fleece Works on a postcard by local photographer Arthur W. Utton. He signed the card in 1915 and sent it to Astwood Bank. Note the World War One recruiting poster on the wall on the right of the picture. The works later became part of Needle Industries but is now demolished.

This 3d brass pub token from the Barley Mow, Studley, was issued by J. Whitehead.

The Barley Mow Hotel in 1905 when the licensee was Mr A. Clarkson.

These houses at the bottom of Fleece Hill opposite the Barley Mow were demolished by Cater's in 1960.

The Baptist Manse, Alcester Road, Studley in about 1910. The picture was taken by Redditch photographer L.L. Sealey.

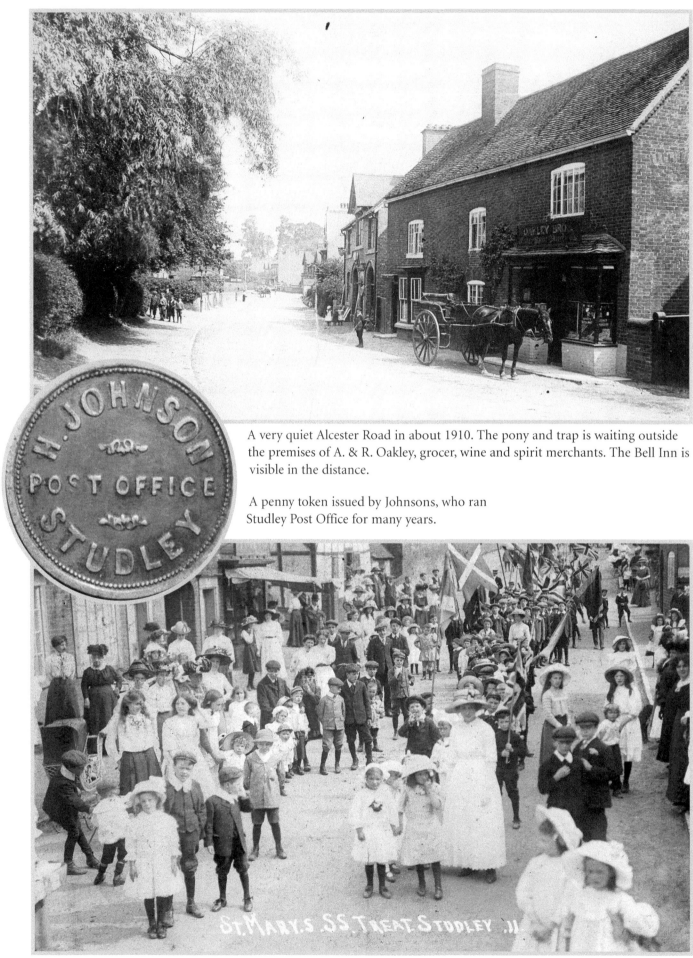

A very quiet Alcester Road in about 1910. The pony and trap is waiting outside the premises of A. & R. Oakley, grocer, wine and spirit merchants. The Bell Inn is visible in the distance.

A penny token issued by Johnsons, who ran Studley Post Office for many years.

A postcard showing St Mary's Sunday School treat, sent on 9 July 1912.

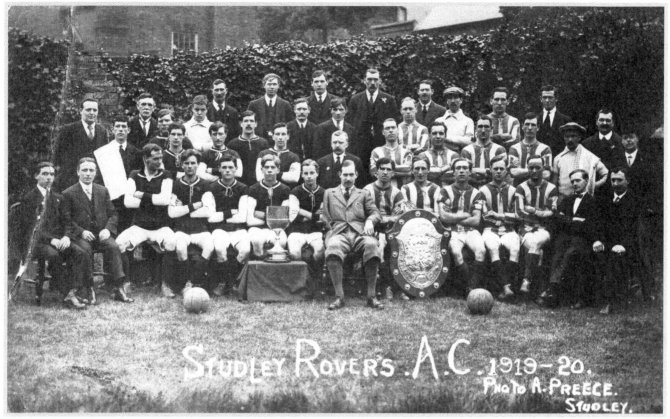

Another Studley photographer took this group photograph in 1920.

The Astwood Bank and Studley station buildings remain but the track has gone.

Morrall's needle factory in Green Lane was known as 'The Towers'. The buildings on the left of this picture have now gone, but the Needlemaker's Arms on the right remains – now called the Griffin Inn.

This 3d pub token from the Needlemaker's Arms, Green Lane, was issued by Abel Morrall and could be from as early as 1850. It gave admittance to the pleasure gardens and bowling green. The pub later became the Griffin Inn.

Studley Castle in Edwardian times when it was a very famous horticultural college for women, founded by the Countess of Warwick.

The castle interior.

A wonderful crop of grapes under glass in 1913.

Studley Vicarage.

A tranquil scene on the banks of the Arrow in 1924.

'Skilts', Mappleborough Green, in 1910 when it was home to Sir W. Jaffray.

Mappleborough Green schools pictured in 1919; the small girl looking over the hedge should, perhaps, be inside the school.

The Dog Inn, Mappleborough Green, as it was in November 1960 – its appearance has changed a little since then.

A couple dressed up for
Gorcott Fete in about 1920.

Gorcott Hall in the 1930s on a postcard published by Tipper
and Smallwood of the Beoley Tea Rooms.